Gangsters

Other Books in the History Makers Series:

*History*MAKERS

Gangsters

By Adam Woog

Lucent Books
P.O. Box 289011, San Diego, CA 92198-9011

For my anonymous source

On Cover: *John Gotti (background) reputed mob boss, arrives at New York Supreme Court, New York City, February 9, 1990. Mobster Meyer Lansky (top right), August 1971. Al Capone (bottom left) being taken into custody in Miami, Florida, 1930s.*

Library of Congress Cataloging-in-Publication Data

Woog, Adam, 1953–
    Gangsters / by Adam Woog.
        p.   cm. — (History makers)
Includes bibliographical references and index.
Summary: Discusses the rise of the American gangster including six famous gangsters: Al Capone, "Lucky" Luciano, Meyer Lansky, Benjamin "Bugsy" Siegel, Sam Giancana, and John Gotti.
    ISBN 1-56006-638-5 (lib. bdg. : alk. paper)
    1. Gangsters—United States—History—20th Century—Juvenile litera- ture. 2. Gangsters—United States—Biography—Juvenile literature
    [1. Gangsters.]
    I. Title.   II. Series.
HV6783 .W66 2000
364.1'06'60973—dc21   99-050754

Printed in the U.S.A.

CONTENTS

FOREWORD

The literary form most often referred to as "multiple biography" was perfected in the first century A.D. by Plutarch, a perceptive and talented moralist and historian who hailed from the small town of Chaeronea in central Greece. His most famous work, *Parallel Lives*, consists of a long series of biographies of noteworthy ancient Greek and Roman statesmen and military leaders. Frequently, Plutarch compares a famous Greek to a famous Roman, pointing out similarities in personality and achievements. These expertly constructed and very readable tracts provided later historians and others, including playwrights like Shakespeare, with priceless information about prominent ancient personages and also inspired new generations of writers to tackle the multiple biography genre.

The Lucent History Makers series proudly carries on the venerable tradition handed down from Plutarch. Each volume in the series consists of a set of five to eight biographies of important and influential historical figures who were linked together by a common factor. In *Rulers of Ancient Rome*, for example, all the figures were generals, consuls, or emperors of either the Roman Republic or Empire; while the subjects of *Fighters Against American Slavery*, though they lived in different places and times, all shared the same goal, namely the eradication of human servitude. Mindful that politicians and military leaders are not (and never have been) the only people who shape the course of history, the editors of the series have also included representatives from a wide range of endeavors, including scientists, artists, writers, philosophers, religious leaders, and sports figures.

Each book is intended to give a range of figures—some well known, others less known; some who made a great impact on history, others who made only a small impact. For instance, by making Columbus's initial voyage possible, Spain's Queen Isabella I, featured in *Women Leaders of Nations*, helped to open up the New World to exploration and exploitation by the European powers. Unarguably, therefore, she made a major contribution to a series of events that had momentous consequences for the entire world. By contrast, Catherine II, the eighteenth-century Russian queen, and Golda Meir, the modern Israeli prime minister, did not play roles of global impact; however, their policies and actions significantly influenced the historical development of both their own countries and their regional neighbors. Regardless of their relative importance in the greater historical scheme, all of the figures chronicled in the History Makers series made contributions to posterity; and their public achievements, as well as what is known about their private lives, are presented and evaluated in light of the most recent scholarship.

In addition, each volume in the series is documented and substantiated by a wide array of primary and secondary source quotations. The primary source quotes enliven the text by presenting eyewitness views of the times and culture in which each history maker lived; while the secondary source quotes, taken from the works of respected modern scholars, offer expert elaboration and/or critical commentary. Each quote is footnoted, demonstrating to the reader exactly where biographers find their information. The footnotes also provide the reader with the means of conducting additional research. Finally, to further guide and illuminate readers, each volume in the series features photographs, two bibliographies, and a comprehensive index.

The History Makers series provides both students engaged in research and more casual readers with informative, enlightening, and entertaining overviews of individuals from a variety of circumstances, professions, and backgrounds. No doubt all of them, whether loved or hated, benevolent or cruel, constructive or destructive, will remain endlessly fascinating to each new generation seeking to identify the forces that shaped their world.

Six Bosses

There's plenty for everyone.
—Al Capone

People have long been fascinated by gangsters—or, at least, by the popular images of gangsters. These images fall into a few broad types.

One is the romantic gangster: a tough-talking, hard-drinking, flashily dressed, womanizing swashbuckler who rules his turf with a strong but fair hand. Another is the comic gangster: the bumbling, dim-witted crook who can't shoot straight. A third is the dour, ruthless thug who impassively consigns all his enemies to the bottom of the nearest river.

The reality of organized crime is quite different. Organized crime is a huge and hugely profitable network of closely interwoven businesses. As shown by the testimony of informers over the years, the average gangster's life is generally no more exciting than that of the average businessman. It varies mostly in the degree to which thuggish, distinctly unromantic violence enters the scene.

Nonetheless, society's fascination and even fondness for gangsters remains. Much of this appeal comes from books and movies—especially movies. Almost since the first motion pictures flickered on a screen, gangster movies have been surefire hits.

The Movie Gangster

Early gangster-movie stars included tough little Edward G. Robinson, who achieved fame with the likes of *Little Caesar*, and smooth George Raft, who starred in *Scarface* and took some tips from his friend, the real-life mobster Ben "Bugsy" Siegel. Raft and Siegel were not the only ones to blur the line between the movies and the underworld; as early as 1928, real-life bootleggers were "technical consultants" on *The Racket*, one of the first of many movies modeled on Al Capone. Writer Albert Mobilio notes, "It's always been hard to say where the movies leave off and the real hoodlums begin."[1]

Many film and crime historians argue that the gangster movie's finest hour came in 1972. *The Godfather* was a masterpiece in which director Francis Coppola turned Mario Puzo's best-selling novel into high art, spinning a tale of epic proportions about a Mafia family. For millions of people, *The Godfather* and its two sequels defined the popular image of gangsters (and, incidentally, introduced the term "godfather" in reference to a crime patriarch, a usage Puzo said he invented).

The delight the public takes in gangsters both real and fictional never seems to wane. Every season sees a flood of new Mob-related movies, novels, biographies, histories, and true-crime books. Albert Mobilio wryly notes, "Indeed, if the Mafia owned a copyright on itself, [its members] wouldn't need to make a killing, except on the book rack. And, of course, at the box office."[2]

The Bosses

A handful of real-life gangsters in American history stand out as colorfully as the fictional gangsters of print and film.

Virtually all were first- or second-generation immigrants, poor men who turned to a life of crime as a means of escape from poverty-stricken lives. Though many were of Italian origin, as a whole they represented a broad spectrum of immigrants. Their associates also came, almost exclusively, from humble immigrant ranks, and many sported colorful names: "Big Tuna" Accardo, "Dasher" Abbandando, "Benny Squint," "Tick Tock" Tannenbaum, "Machine Gun" Jack McGurn, Frank "The Enforcer" Nitti.

Though the lives of the men in this book sometimes overlap, each is distinctive enough to warrant individual attention. Taken together, they represent the rise and fall of the underworld, American style—and serve as a prelude to the current crop of crime lords who come from more recently arrived immigrant groups.

The notorious gangster, Al "Scarface" Capone, was and still is strongly associated with Chicago.

9

Al Capone: The King of Chicago

As Houdini is for magic, Al "Scarface" Capone (1899–1947) is synonymous with organized crime. Within the space of a dozen violent years, Capone rose from obscure hoodlum to being the absolute ruler of his city's criminal empire during the heyday of Prohibition. Writer Sidney Zion states, "Capone, in his twenties, ran Chicago like a Roman emperor."[3] His downfall at the hands of the Internal Revenue Service was as swift as his rise.

Capone's reputation has remained so closely linked with his adopted hometown that, even today, people in distant parts of the world will cheerfully pretend to fire a machine gun when they hear the word "Chicago." In his own way, Capone has become as familiar an icon as any other American figure from this century. Biographer Robert J. Schoenberg writes, "Al Capone was, beyond question, the world's best-known gangster, and one of the best-known Americans."[4]

Lucky Luciano: The Organizer

In the 1930s, Salvatore Lucania, better known as Lucky Luciano (1897–1962), dominated the drug trade in America after World War II. Even more importantly to the history of the underworld, Luciano revolutionized the way crime was committed in America. Prior to the 1930s, criminals operated within relatively small boundaries and geographical areas.

Luciano was the primary force in creating from these geographically separate groups a streamlined national organization commonly known as the Syndicate or the Mob. This new order joined crime figures from all over the country into a far-reaching, tightly organized and strictly controlled invisible government.

Because of his role in creating this network, Luciano is considered by some authorities to be the single most important figure in organized crime's history. Journalist Rhymer Rigby states, "Lucky Luciano's transformation of the Mafia in the U.S. into a streamlined operation in the 1930s established it as one the most effective criminal empires the world has known."[5]

Meyer Lansky: Quiet Banker to the Mob

Although he preferred to shun the spotlight, unlike some of his more flamboyant colleagues, Meyer Lansky (1902–1983) was the most famous of the many Jewish gangsters who flourished during Prohibition and in the years after. He began as a bootlegger, became a key element in Luciano's national crime syndicate, and later served as the Mob's chief banker. His personal fortune was built on a vast, international string of gambling casinos. Late in life, he became interested in the state of Israel and tried unsuccessfully to immigrate to that country.

A major reason for Lansky's success was his shrewd intelligence and gift for numbers; he is considered by some biographers to have been a near genius, and they acknowledge that Lansky would have excelled at anything if circumstances had been different. Journalist Pete Hamill writes, "In a different era, he might have been successful in almost any business. But Lansky and his [friends] were unwilling to serve long apprenticeships or live humble lives of self-sacrifice. They were drawn instead to the rackets."[6]

The brilliant Meyer Lansky, who avoided the limelight, made his fortune through gambling casinos.

Benjamin "Bugsy" Siegel: The Man Who Invented Las Vegas

Benjamin Siegel (1906–1947) was the most dashing of the dashing, playboy gangsters. Siegel's flamboyant style was markedly different from those of his lifelong friends, the conservative Luciano and the reclusive Lansky. He first made his mark in Los Angeles as a handsome "sportsman" who hung out with movie stars and was mentioned frequently in the gossip columns.

Siegel's grand obsession—building a lavish casino in the desert—both made him famous and caused his violent downfall. Strictly speaking, Siegel did not invent Las Vegas as a gambling mecca; it had been there before him. He did, however, see its potential for glamour and greatness, and it is thanks to him that Vegas is famous today. Pete Hamill writes,

> Las Vegas is his truest monument. . . . That garish skyline, those ten thousand blinking, popping, humming electric signs defying the night, defying time's passage, were imagined first by Ben Siegel. Today, the signs, the casinos, the millions of visitors are proof of the creed by which Siegel lived his short and dangerous life: Sin is more profitable than virtue.[7]

Sam Giancana: Strongman with a Presidential Connection

Sam "Mooney" Giancana (1908–1975) was for many years the crime boss of Chicago. But his career also reached deep into organized crime around the world, with complex connections to a wide variety of figures like labor organizer Jimmy Hoffa as well as celebrities from Hollywood and Washington, D.C.

Benjamin Siegel was obsessed with the idea of turning a desert into a luxurious casino.

The love of Giancana's life was a famous singer, Phyllis McGuire. Frank Sinatra and Marilyn Monroe were two of his many friends. Giancana also apparently had close ties to the Central Intelligence Agency (CIA). Furthermore, evidence points to a bizarre love triangle involving Giancana, a young woman named Judith Campbell, and John F. Kennedy, then the president of the United States.

There is no definitive proof that Giancana was closely allied to the CIA, John Kennedy, and other government figures. However, the evidence is strong, and to many observers the gangster was clearly at the center of an elaborate web of deep intrigue connecting government agents and the underworld. "It's beautiful," Giancana once reportedly boasted. "The Outfit even has the same enemies as the government."[8]

John Gotti: The Teflon Don

John J. Gotti (1940–) was the world's best-known gangster in the 1980s. Until 1992, Gotti was the so-called boss of bosses

John J. Gotti headed one of the most important Mafia-related crime families of New York.

of the Gambino family, one of the most important Mafia-related crime families of New York. A tough street brawler who rose to the top through tenacity and violence, in his later years Gotti became an impeccably dressed media celebrity known as the Dapper Don.

Many observers feel that Gotti was the last truly powerful figure in a Mafia crippled by deep-reaching investigations and the incarceration of dozens of top criminals. Gotti himself was sentenced to life in jail in 1992, putting to rest another nickname—the Teflon Don—bestowed on him for his ability to keep criminal charges from sticking. To many, Gotti was the last of the great Mafia chiefs. However, some observers feel otherwise; according to Joseph Coffey, a senior investigator with New York State's organized crime task force, "The Mob will never be finished as long as there's a dollar to be made."[9]

Organized crime has been a part of the fabric of society for generations, and its roots stretch back hundreds of years. The stories of these six gangsters—and of the environment in which they thrived—form a vital part of American history.

CHAPTER 1

The Rise of the American Gangster

Americans thought [that with Prohibition] they could legislate morals; instead, they created the Mob.

—Journalist Pete Hamill

Organized crime has existed for centuries, in various forms and in many parts of the world. Its most visible form, however, has been the vast illegal business conglomerate that arose in the United States late in the 1800s, flourished in the middle decades of the twentieth century, and still exists today.

This organization largely replaced (both in reality and in the public's imagination) older-style American criminals, who tended to operate alone or in small, independent gangs. Among the most famous of these were the James brothers, Frank and Jesse, who operated in the years after the Civil War, and depression-era bank robbers such as John Dillinger, Bonnie Parker and Clyde Barrow, and "Pretty Boy" Floyd. As the twentieth century progressed, however, lone desperadoes found it harder and harder to work without the cooperation of the larger, more organized criminal entities.

This underworld of organized crime has gone by many names: the Syndicate, the Mob, and the Organization are only three. One of the most common names

Bonnie Parker and Clyde Barrow were famous bank robbers during the depression era.

for it is the Mafia. This term, however, is something of a misnomer. Accurately used, the word "Mafia" refers to a very specific fraternal organization. Furthermore, although the Mafia has indeed played a key role in organized crime's history, it is only one part of the story.

The Mafia

Many ethnic groups have had certain members who have had their fingers in American organized crime at some time or another. One of these was the Italian-American community.

At the turn of the century, many Italian immigrants came to America seeking work. A good percentage came from Sicily, a hard-bitten agricultural island with a long and distinguished history. Sicily had for centuries been desperately poor and oppressed by the mainland government. Tyrannical officials, dishonest tax collectors, corrupt judges, and greedy landlords ruthlessly exploited its peasant population.

This population of otherwise honest people, fearing that it could not trust the government, often turned to the bosses of local criminal gangs for protection or justice. The bosses gradually became respected and powerful figures in their communities. As the bosses became more powerful, law-abiding citizens often found themselves deeply in debt, financially or otherwise, to the Mafia, as the criminal organization was called, as a result of "favors" its leaders provided.

Italian immigrants who arrived in America after the Civil War brought with them this centuries-old distrust of authority. They

America's big cities attracted immigrants who sought promise of work in a new city.

15

came to places like New York, Chicago, and New Orleans in search of work as fishermen, longshoremen, and merchants. A small percentage of immigrants, inevitably, were petty criminals and members of the Mafia. The Mafia members brought with them their traditions of violence, strict codes of conduct, secrecy, and brotherhood.

They operated mostly within their own tightly knit communities. For instance, they might extort money from someone by sending threatening letters. Such a note was commonly signed *mano nera*—"black hand"—and accompanied by a drawing of a black hand. This name and symbol later came to represent Italian gangsters.

A notorious murder helped bring the immigrant underworld to the public eye as it caused an international uproar. In 1890, New Orleans' police chief was fatally shot outside his home, and it was widely assumed that the murderers were Italian. Over one hundred men were arrested and nine were put on trial.

The evidence was slight, however, and the jury acquitted them. Angered at the verdict, a mob broke into the jail and lynched eleven Italian prisoners. A furious Italian government recalled its ambassador to America in protest,j and even considered declaring war. The crisis was resolved when the United States agreed to pay twenty-five thousand dollars to compensate the victims' families.

Other Ethnic Influences

Another ethnic group contributing to the Mob's development was the Irish. One prominent Irish gangster was Dion O'Banion, the so-called beer baron of Chicago during Prohibition. Ironically, as Irish immigrants became assimilated into American life, they became closely linked with police forces across the country. Joining the police force, passing the tradition from one family member to another, became an important part of Irish-American life.

Jews were still another key ethnic group. Due to an influx of Jews from Germany, the nation's Jewish population rose from fifty-thousand in 1860 to a quarter million by 1880. A far larger contingent came around the turn of the century; between 1881 and 1914, some 2 million eastern European Jews entered the country.

Despite a reputation for being a group that avoided wrong-doing, it was inevitable that a few criminals would be part of this massive arrival. Historian Robert A. Rockaway notes, "From their earliest residence in the United States, dating back to the mid–seventeenth century, Jews had enjoyed a reputation for being among the country's most law-abiding and least violent citizens. . . . This spotless reputation began to tarnish in the nineteenth century."[10]

By the turn of the century, the reputation was definitely tarnished. Probably the most famous of all the Jewish gangsters in the days before organized crime really blossomed was Arnold Rothstein, a suave, dapper gambler and drug trafficker. Rothstein pioneered the permanent transformation of American crime, from petty larceny into big business, that Meyer Lansky, Lucky Luciano, and "Bugsy" Siegel later perfected. In the words of historian Jill Jonnes, Rothstein was "an all-around criminal genius, one whose prodigious energy, imagination, and intellect had catapulted him to supremacy in an underworld that he changed forever."[11]

"The Brain"

Rothstein, the son of pious Orthodox Jews, rejected his parents' lifestyle and cultivated instead a dapper image of himself as the unofficial "mayor" of New York's Broadway. (His nickname, "The Brain," was given to him by Damon Runyon, the writer who created the Broadway characters of *Guys and Dolls*.) He raised thoroughbred horses, enjoyed the company of glamorous women, flashed huge cash bankrolls, and tooled around New York in a chauffeured Rolls-Royce.

This lavish style was based on thinking big. In an era when others were still working small, traditional rackets, Rothstein created a million-dollar stolen-bond business; pioneered the

Arnold "The Brain" Rothstein was involved in many illicit activities—including drug trafficking.

first liquor smuggling into America during the years it was illegal; cultivated illicit relationships between criminals and politicians on a level never before imagined; and brought blackmail to sophisticated new heights through the use of extensive labor racketeering, a process that threatened strikes and walkouts. It is also widely believed that Rothstein was the force behind the infamous fixing of the 1919 World Series. One criminal enterprise, however, stands as Rothstein's most enduring legacy: large-scale, international drug trafficking.

American authorities had realized early in the century that they had a fast-spreading drug problem, especially in urban slums. In 1914, Congress passed a narcotic act designed to restrict access to morphine, cocaine, and heroin. By the mid-1920s, American pharmaceutical firms no longer were able to easily manufacture and market the opiate and cocaine products that had once been common. But the demand was still there, and Rothstein seized the opportunity to smuggle large shipments of drugs from Europe or Asia. Heroin and other narcotics could be purchased easily from legitimate pharmaceutical firms there, with no questions asked, then smuggled quietly into America.

Using a mortgage company as a false "front" business, Rothstein not only ran the smuggling; he arranged a vast network to distribute his product as well. His other businesses provided the capital; his cozy relationships with politicians ensured his operation's continuance; and his close connections with criminal gangs across America ensured thorough distribution.

As a result, the amounts of smuggled drugs seized by federal customs agents increased year by year. For the fiscal year ending in mid-1926, U.S. Customs agents confiscated 449 pounds of opium, 42 pounds of morphine, 3.5 pounds of heroin, and 10 pounds of cocaine. Two years later, those figures had soared to 2,354 pounds of opium, 91 pounds of morphine, 27 pounds of heroin, and 30 pounds of cocaine. And that, needless to say, was only what was captured.

Rothstein managed to evade prosecution for years. He admitted he had lent money to drug traffickers, but insisted he had no idea what they were doing with it. Authorities failed to prove he had any more direct connection to the ring. Before they could build a sufficient case, the gangster was assassinated, in 1928 at the age of forty-six. No one was ever indicted for Rothstein's murder, although most crime historians conclude that

Crime historians speculate that John "Legs" Diamond (pictured) was responsible for the murder of Rothstein.

it was the work of another gangster, John "Legs" Diamond, who was angered over a double cross.

Prohibition Roars In

Several aspects of organized crime were already in place by the time Rothstein came along. The term "gangsters" had sprung up in the mid-1800s to describe bands of thieves. Around the same time, systematic cooperation between criminals and politicians began in the major cities. The concept of protection—paying money to ensure that nothing bad happened to people or property—was also solidly established in such places as the nation's docks and gambling houses.

Until about 1920, however, American crime was a disorganized affair, conducted by a motley collection of small-time villains who had operated almost completely within their own tightly knit neighborhoods. That year, everything changed. Criminals were offered a hugely profitable, completely irresistable opportunity to expand their operations into national and even international concerns. The opportunity was called Prohibition.

"Prohibition" was the term for an amendment to the U.S. Constitution that banned the manufacture, sale, or transportation of intoxicating alcohol. A "dry" nation had been the dream of anti-alcohol forces since the Civil War, and it became reality in 1920 with the passage of the Volstead Act, which defined how the amendment would be enforced. However, the plan backfired dramatically. Many Americans liked to drink, they were determined to drink, and they were willing to go to great lengths and expense to drink. As politicians and police authorities quickly discovered, many Americans were also willing to break the law to drink.

The nation's gangsters were delighted to accommodate the public's needs. "Bootlegging," as the illegal trade in alcohol was called, quickly rose to the top of the list of criminal activities. Journalist Jack Kelly writes, "With the advent of Prohibition, bootlegging became the chief gangster priority. Jostling for territory began as soon as the Volstead Act took effect."[12]

The Roaring Twenties

Gangsters lost no time in setting up hidden bars, called "speakeasies," and "blind pigs"—grocery or hardware stores that secretly doubled as taverns. At the more lavish of these, customers could drink, gamble, and dance or listen to music. Liquor supplies came from hidden distilleries or were smuggled in from overseas. The 1920s are often called the Roaring Twenties, and much of that roar was made in illegal speakeasies over "bathtub gin" and "needle beer" (nonalcoholic near beer with added alcohol or ether).

The risks were great. Bloody gang wars, product hijackings, and rubouts (as the press called underworld murders) became common. It has been estimated that more than a thousand gang-related killings took place in New York City alone during the Roaring Twenties.

However, the potential profits were worth the risk. Just in Chicago, for instance, Al Capone's gang grossed an estimated $60 million a year—an astonishing fortune in 1920s dollars. The side benefits were exciting, too, at least in the public eye: newspapers portrayed the underworld as a glittering realm of swank nightclubs, well-dressed bosses, fearless gunmen, and glamorous women—a world where fortunes could be made and lost overnight.

To many regular citizens, gangsters were charismatic folk heroes, not criminals but simply businessmen who supplied a needed service. Journalist Sidney Zion writes,

> Most people saw the mobsters as lovable rogues. . . . The Mob provided millions of satisfied customers with everything from hooch to theater tickets. They lent cash when the banks said no. They provided businessmen with the unions of choice and the unions with the goons of their choice, [and they] gave us Las Vegas, the point spread and double-breasted pin-stripe suits.[13]

Post-Prohibition

Many police authorities hoped that the end of Prohibition in 1933 would deal a blow to organized crime. However, a number of gangsters had already seen the legalization of alcohol coming, and they made sure that their businesses had already expanded profitably into other areas.

Some preferred to focus on shifting into traditionally illegal areas such as prostitution, gambling, and narcotics. Another area that opened up for gangsters during the post-Prohibition years was labor racketeering. The economic slump of the Great Depression, which began in 1929, created extreme tensions between America's laboring and management classes. Employers and labor union leaders alike often tried to antagonize their opponents with lockouts, strikes, and outright workplace battles. Gangsters found they could profit in this explosive arena, first as hired muscle and then in other ways.

Revelers celebrate the end of Prohibition in 1933. By then, many gangsters had already begun to focus on other profitable illegal activities.

In New York, for instance, racketeers (as such gangsters were called) gained control of unions controlling such businesses as garment factories, fish markets, bakeries, taxi fleets, and dockworkers. They played both sides, ransacking the welfare funds of the unions and extorting management with threatened strikes or arson.

Other gangsters preferred to move into legitimate businesses, such as importing, running legal distilleries, and operating liquor distributorships. These last were simply a logical next step; at a 1929 underworld conference in Atlantic City, Lucky Luciano reportedly remarked, "After all, who knows more about the liquor business than us?"[14]

Organization

Prohibition had given gangsters a reason to organize, so they could handle the widespread manufacture, distribution, and sales of liquor. In the years following the repeal of Prohibition, the need for tight organization became even greater.

In the 1930s, a group of gangsters from around the country, spearheaded by Lucky Luciano, formed a national syndicate. By the middle of the decade, this organization was a well-established machine. Franchises for enterprises in a given city were apportioned by a national committee. If violence was necessary, approval was needed from this national level. Activities were overseen by regional bosses who reported to higher-up officers. It was possible for someone to rise within the organization by virtue of talent and effort. Differences were settled by arbitration whenever possible.

Many of the fundamental ideas behind this well-run organization had been first seen in Arnold Rothstein's blending of business and crime. For instance, Rothstein had perfected the alliance between gangsters and politicians, in the belief that crime was a business like any other. Other Rothstein rules for success echoed capitalism's fundamental ideas: spend money to make money; give the customers what they want; image is important, so dress well, use good manners, keep your word, and recruit intelligently.

These lessons were taken to heart by the new generation. Above all, Rothstein counseled, avoid public violence and attention; they are always bad for business. As Al Capone told reporters, "There is enough business for all of us without killing each other like animals in the streets."[15]

Flourishing

Over the years, many government agents and agencies have done their best to expose and destroy elements of organized crime. These have included Prohibition-era agents like Eliot Ness, whose team of federal agents became known as "The Untouchables" because of their resistance to bribery, as well as many other police and federal agents in the 1940s, 1950s, and more recent times.

Some of the most significant federal crackdowns have included the Senate crime committees of the 1950s and 1960s, such as the Kefauver and McClellan Commissions. Their efforts at exposing the highly organized structure of crime in America were eye-openers to an America that had been led to believe that no such thing as the Mob existed.

In part, this relative innocence was due to J. Edgar Hoover, the powerful, longtime head of the Federal Bureau of Investigation; Hoover insisted for many years that organized crime was a myth, and he persisted in tracking individual criminals rather than in creating a systematic hunt. One of the best-known of all anticrime figures during this era, and often a staunch foe of Hoover, was Robert F. Kennedy, then the attorney general in his brother John's White House administration.

Eliot Ness (right), a member of a team of federal agents known as "The Untouchables," fought against organized crime.

One of the crime-fighters' strongest allies, meanwhile, was a midlevel mobster named Joseph Valachi, who in 1962 decided to inform on his colleagues and tell what he knew to government agents. Much of what Valachi said was ridiculed by organized crime mobsters, and the veracity of some of his testimony has since been questioned by authorities. Nonetheless, Valachi's decision to go against the Mob was a groundbreaking move that paved the way for more recent informants, such as John Gotti's right-hand man, Sammy "The Bull" Gravano.

The Kefauver and McClellan Commissions and other anti-crime investigations of the 1950s and 1960s exposed to the public, for the first time, a carefully assembled, tightly knit, highly secret organization. According to their research, the power within the underworld had largely been assumed by Italian-American gangsters, while the power of other ethnic groups had lessened considerably.

Our Thing

This underworld revolved around several major and minor crime "families," organized along the traditional lines of the Sicilian Mafia. Members of these families were not necessarily blood relations, but each swore allegiance to his individual family. A member who proved his loyalty by killing a member of a rival organization in an approved execution was referred to as a "made man" and accepted into the highest level of the organization via an elaborate ceremony. According to Valachi's testimony, another name for this group was *La Cosa Nostra*—literally, "our thing." Many sources claim that such nicknames are largely the invention of the media. Nonetheless, they have stuck, along with other aspects of Valachi's assertions. This testimony, for better or worse, did much to cement in the popular imagination the image of the Italian-American gangster.

In more recent years, federal prosecutors have been more successful than their earlier counterparts at tracking down and imprisoning mob figures. In the 1970s, a powerful law called RICO (Racketeer Influenced and Corrupt Organizations Act) was passed. It has allowed authorities to put behind bars virtually all of the heads of the most powerful crime families. While this has seriously crippled the old-style mob, organized crime continues to exist. Meanwhile, more recent ethnic groups have entered the fray, creating their own, newer versions of organized crime and ensuring that the efforts of law enforcement authorities are far from over.

The Prohibition years and the three or four decades after could be considered a kind of "golden era" for organized crime—the period when it formed, blossomed, and was at its most powerful peak. The Mob during those years was led by a handful of singularly ruthless gangsters who mixed legitimate business with violent crime. The most famous of them all was the iron-fisted king of Chicago: Al Capone.

CHAPTER 2

Al Capone: The King of Chicago

When I sell liquor, they call it bootlegging. When my patrons serve it on silver trays on Lake Shore Drive, they call it hospitality.
—Al Capone

Gabriel Capone, a barber from Naples, arrived in New York with his wife Teresa shortly before the beginning of the twentieth century, part of the huge wave of immigrants that was flooding America. They settled in a tough, working-class neighborhood of Brooklyn populated by a diverse mix of immigrants, including Swedes, Irish, Jews, and Italians.

Their fourth child, Alphonse, was born in Brooklyn on January 17, 1899. Some sources list his birth name as Caponi, but the correct spelling was always Capone; the discrepancy arose because the pronunciation in Italian is *Capon-ay*. The gangster later anglicized the pronunciation of his name to *Ca-pōn*.

Capone's interest in school slackened as he was drawn to crime.

Childhood

Capone was a bright child who maintained a B average throughout grade school. As he grew older he grew husky, always more interested in playing baseball than in his studies. He had to repeat the sixth grade because he was truant so often. When Capone was fourteen, he struck a female teacher and was in turn beaten by the school principal. That was the end of his formal education.

He began a succession of regular jobs, including clerking in a candy store, but he was drawn to the crime that was rampant in his neighborhood. He joined the Brooklyn contingent of the Five Points Gang, which specialized in protection—that is, extorting money from businessmen in return for leaving their shops alone. The beefy teenager, known for his temper and penchant for violence, was a natural when a pushcart owner or other "client" needed a violent lesson in what happened if protection money was not paid. Rumors that Capone killed two men by the age of eighteen have not been substantiated.

When he was nineteen, Capone married Mary Coughlin, a pretty blond he had met at a dance. Mae, as she was called, was also a child of immigrants—in her case, from Ireland. Just before the wedding, she gave birth to Alphonse Junior, nicknamed Sonny.

Two leaders of the Five Points Gang were Frankie Yale and Johnny Torrio. Each would play a major role in Capone's development as a gangster. Crime historian William Bolsano notes, "Capone served his apprenticeship in organized crime at the knee of Frankie Yale."[16] And Capone himself once remarked, "I looked on Johnny like my adviser and father."[17]

New York to Chicago

While working as a bouncer and bartender in one of Yale's clubs, Capone acquired the disfigurement that inspired his nickname, "Scarface." The three prominent scars on his cheek were not the result of military bravery, as Capone later claimed; when Capone insulted the sister of another Brooklyn thug, the furious brother jumped over the bar with a knife.

After Capone wounded another gangster in a brawl, he needed to lie low. Yale suggested moving to Chicago, where their old friend Johnny Torrio had moved to help his cousin, local hoodlum "Big Jim" Colosimo. Late in 1919, the Capones moved west, and Al found work as a bartender and bouncer at the Four Deuces, Colosimo's lavish night spot.

Torrio had become Colosimo's business manager, and when Prohibition came in he was eager to begin bootlegging. However, Colosimo was satisfied with the way things were. He resisted bootlegging and wanted only to become a respectable restaurant owner. The tension between the two men was resolved when Colosimo was gunned down outside his office. The murderer's identity was never established, although evidence points to Frankie Yale.

With Colosimo's death, Torrio became one of the city's top gangland leaders. His friend Capone was the natural choice to become his right-hand man. Capone created a front for himself, a phony business operation that masked his true activities. He listed himself in the phone book as a used furniture dealer, and even printed up cards: "Alphonse Capone, Second Hand Furniture Dealer, 2220 South Wabash Avenue."[18]

Death in a Flower Shop

From 1920 to 1923, the Chicago underworld was relatively peaceful. Capone and Torrio reached agreements with most of the other gangs about the division of territories and operations.

The major dividing line was between the city's north and south sides. Torrio and Capone had the south; an Irishman, Dion "Deanie" O'Banion, had the north. O'Banion, a native of the hard-bitten North Side neighborhood called Little Hell, was a brutal killer who may have committed as many as two dozen murders. But he also had a surprising passion for flowers and owned a half-interest in a florist's shop, where he spent many hours working on arrangements.

The peace between O'Banion and the Torrio-Capone outfit lasted until 1924. Angered over an apparent double cross, Torrio arranged for three men to visit O'Banion in his flower shop. One shook O'Banion's hand, preventing him from reaching for any of his three pistols, while the others pumped bullets into him.

Although Torrio and Capone tried to make peace with the remaining North Side gang, all-out war erupted after O'Banion's funeral. One attack severely wounded Torrio and convinced him to retire. His operations went into the hands of twenty-five-year-old Capone. Though it was widely accepted that Hymie Weiss, one of O'Banion's lieutenants, led the attack on Torrio, Lucky Luciano later claimed

The murder of Dion O'Banion (pictured) instigated a gang war between the north and south side of Chicago.

that Capone himself ordered the hit: "He tried to eliminate Johnny the same way Johnny done with Colosimo."[19]

Shortly afterwards, ten cars sped past a crowded restaurant where Capone was eating lunch and riddled the place with machine guns and shotguns. Miraculously, only four people were wounded and none killed. Two weeks later, Capone retaliated: Hymie Weiss was struck down in a hail of machine-gun fire.

Although Capone rarely carried a gun himself and publicly denounced violence, he guarded himself thoroughly. A writer for the *New Yorker* magazine noted that

> Al travels in a bullet-proof car. He surrounds himself with eight men selected for thickness of torso who form an inner ring about him when he appears in public. They are tall and he is short, a precaution against any attempt to aim at him through the spaces between their necks. For Al's protection, the eight men wear bullet-proof vests. Nothing smaller than a fieldpiece could penetrate his double-walled fortress of meat.[20]

Corruption

As he tightened his grip on bootlegging, Capone branched out into other activities, including prostitution, gambling, and labor racketeering. He formed phony associations for soda pop peddlers, motion picture operators, even Jewish poultry workers. These alleged unions extorted money from businesses by threatening strikes or violence. Capone also developed a milk distribution company, and was delighted to discover that milk had a bigger markup than alcohol: "Honest to God, we've been in the wrong racket right along."[21]

Capone's activities thrived because of systems that ensured cooperation: inspectors who looked the other way, judges and juries who were bribed or intimidated, police who arrested only rival gangs. Historian Michael Woodiwiss writes, "The Capone syndicate was only able to function . . . because of an intricate and enormously expensive link to Chicago's City Hall, involving officials at all levels."[22]

The most flagrant example was William Hale Thompson Jr., the charming millionaire grandson of one of the city's founders and a man commonly referred to as "Capone's mayor." Author Sidney Zion calls "Big Bill" Thompson "probably the most corrupt politician the nation has ever seen."[23]

In 1923, "Big Bill" was replaced with a mayor who promised to clean up the city. During this period of reform, Capone moved to the more lenient suburb of Cicero. Capone fixed the Cicero mayoral elections in favor of his candidate and set up offices in the elegant Hawthorne Inn, using its smoke shop as a front. There was virtually no crime on the streets of Cicero; few crooks had the nerve to tread on Capone's turf. He was also lavish with gifts to the community, and many considered him more Robin Hood than evil criminal.

During the dark days of the depression, for instance, Capone sponsored free soup kitchens that fed thousands each day. He paid for surgery to repair the eyesight of an innocent bystander injured during a gang shootout. He was also known to tip waiters with hundred-dollar bills. Robert J. Schoenberg comments, "In Cicero, Capone ended up as a hero to many."[24]

Cicero to Chicago

Four years after being ousted from the mayor's office, with the help of hundreds of thousands in campaign funds from the Capone organization, "Big Bill" Thompson was re-elected. Capone quietly shifted his headquarters back to Chicago, taking over two floors of the Lexington Hotel.

Capone was now the picture of a busy executive. He sat behind a desk piled high with papers as phones rang constantly. His days were occupied with decision-making, administrative details, and monitoring returns on his investments. He was aided by associates

Capone sponsored free soup kitchens during the depression.

such as his accountant, Jake "Greasy Thumb" Guzik, and his chief of operations, Frank "The Enforcer" Nitti.

He was now as much business owner as gangster, and Capone always thought of himself as a businessman and a patriotic American. "My rackets are run along strict American lines," he once commented. "This American system of ours, call it capitalism, call it what you like—gives each and every one of us a great opportunity if we only seize it with both hands and make the most of it."[25]

Capone spent most days at the Lexington, and often slept there. Officially, however, he lived in the house he had bought upon arriving in Chicago, a modest but large brick house in one of the city's solidly middle-class neighborhoods. Capone's neighbors there often saw him coming and going in his seven-ton armored limousine.

But they also saw Capone play Santa every Christmas at his sister's school, and they witnessed the Capone family worshiping at nearby St. Columbanus Catholic Church. Reporters were once greeted by the criminal monarch in a pink apron at his front door: he had been cooking spaghetti sauce.

Besides Mae, Sonny, and Capone's mother, Capone's two sisters and his brother Ralph lived there. Another brother, Frank, had been killed during one of the periodic gang wars, and Capone's father had died in 1920. Capone's eldest brother, Vincenzo, had distanced himself from the family and moved to the Southwest; as Richard "Two-Gun" Hart, he became a government agent in charge of Indian affairs and Prohibition.

The Big Fellow

Capone could well afford to maintain his large household. The Internal Revenue Service (IRS) estimated Capone's personal profit for 1927 alone at $10 million.

Capone spent much of this wealth on himself. He liked to dress well, in silk suits, spats, and Borsalino fedoras. Friends called him "Snorky"—slang for stylish. (No one called him "Scarface" if they wanted to stay healthy.) He drank expensive liquor, snorted so much cocaine that his septum became perforated, enjoyed the company of teenage girls from his brothels, and gambled extravagantly, boasting of losing $100,000 on a single roll of the dice.

This extravagance, as well as his soup kitchens and other public services, kept Capone in the limelight. Capone became a celebrity; busloads of onlookers drove past his headquarters, hoping to catch a glimpse.

Capone loved the attention. He began holding press conferences to explain his positions on various affairs. He appeared on the cover of *Time*, approached New York publishers about an autobiography, and even toyed with becoming a radio evangelist. When a Russian politician denounced him as an example of capitalism run amuck, Capone boasted that he was known all over the world.

Newspaper reporters loved "the Big Fellow," as they called him. Capone was colorful, talkative, and generous, and stories about him always sold papers. He was uneducated but eloquent, with shrewd opinions on many subjects. He was especially interested in music; he once remarked, "I'm nuts about music. Music makes me forget I'm Al Capone and lifts me up until I think I'm only a block or two from heaven."[26]

The St. Valentine's Day Massacre

By early 1929, the North Side gang was in the hands of George "Bugsy" Moran. Moran was erratic and ineffective, but he still managed to cause trouble for Capone. Far from accepting Capone's requests for a peaceful settlement, he arranged for an attack that wounded Capone's chief bodyguard, "Machine Gun" Jack McGurn. This was probably the trigger for the most infamous mass killing in mob history: the St. Valentine's Day Massacre.

When a group of gangsters offered Moran a bargain-priced shipment of expensive Canadian whiskey they claimed was hijacked from Capone, he was delighted and agreed to oversee delivery personally. The date was set: February 14, 1929.

That morning, seven men gathered at the S.M.C. Cartage Company, a depot for Moran's bootlegging. Six were Moran associates; the seventh was a young man who enjoyed the thrill of hanging out with hoodlums. Before Moran arrived, a police car stopped in front of the building. Two men in uniform and two in plainclothes entered the building and lined up Moran's men along a wall.

Moran's men had no reason to believe this was anything other than a nuisance raid by

George "Bugsy" Moran (pictured) was the chief target of the infamous St. Valentine's Day Massacre.

31

cops who could be easily bought off. A later police statement asserted, "The seven men thought they were facing only arrest. . . . Otherwise [they] would have sold their lives dearly."[27]

However, the "police" opened fire with machine guns and shotguns. The two men in uniform then marched the two in plainclothes back to their car, as if arresting them, and disappeared.

Who Did It?

No one was ever convicted for the murders. Some observers speculated that it was the work of policemen who had a grudge against Moran. Others thought that it was one faction of the Moran gang bent on destroying another. To Moran, however, the answer was clear: "Only Capone kills like that!"[28]

Most crime historians agree that Capone, who was vacationing at his winter estate in Florida, authorized the hit. Almost certainly, the operation was led by "Machine Gun" McGurn. McGurn was spotted in a nearby park that morning, and at least one witness claimed to have seen him outside the S.M.C. garage. However, McGurn claimed he had spent the day with his glamorous girlfriend, Louise Rolfe—"The Blonde Alibi," in the words of the press.

Moran's role in Chicago crime declined in later years, and he was eventually reduced to petty burglary. However, he did apparently manage one last act of vengeance. Seven years after the massacre, unknown gunmen cut "Machine Gun" McGurn down in a bowling alley. They left a comic Valentine card on the body.

Capone's chief bodyguard, "Machine Gun" McGurn, is thought to have led the St. Valentine's Day attack.

The Untouchables

When the Great Depression hit America late in 1929, millions of people were starving and unemployed. Citizens were increasingly less inclined to tolerate flamboyant gangsters and corrupt politicians. Someone needed to be taught a lesson, and Capone was an obvious target. Historian Michael Woodiwiss writes, "The federal administration of President Herbert Hoover was committed to a show of effective liquor-law enforcement and someone had to pay the price. Capone's national notoriety ensured that only he could fit the bill properly."[29]

Helping in the effort to bring down Capone were several government agents. The most famous of these were Eliot Ness and his team of Prohibition agents, the Untouchables, so called for their legendary resistance to bribery. In his memoirs, Ness paints a heroic self-portrait while describing his war against Capone. He vividly calls the Chicago of 1929 "a city ruled by the knife, pistol, shotgun, tommygun and 'pineapple' [hand grenade] of the underworld, a jungle of steel and concrete clutched fast in the fat, diamond-studded hand of a scar-faced killer named Al Capone."[30]

Despite the publicity and the legends, however, the Untouchables' successes were tiny compared to the extent of Capone's vast operations. It is estimated that during the first half of 1930 Chicago bootleggers lost about $1 million in revenues due to Untouchable raids; this was less than four percent of what the bootleggers were handing out just in bribes.

Bringing "The Big Fellow" Down

Other attempts to slow Capone were equally ineffective. His only arrests were minor, the most serious being one for carrying a concealed weapon in Philadelphia that earned him ten months in prison. What finally captured Capone was a relatively mild crime: income tax evasion.

Since the vast majority of his income was illegal, Capone had not bothered to pay taxes in years. In 1928, the Internal Revenue Service received permission to target the gangster and several of his colleagues for evading their income on gambling. Since Capone did not have property in his own name and avoided using banks, checks, or receipts, making a case against him was difficult.

However, the IRS could prove that the Hawthorne Smoke Shop, Capone's front in Cicero, was a gambling den that took in millions yearly. Capone's share of the Hawthorne profits between 1924 and 1928 amounted to over $1 million. This was illegal income, but the IRS argued that it was still taxable and that the gangster owed about a quarter of a million dollars.

A number of celebrities attended Capone's 1931 trial on this charge. One was Edward G. Robinson, the actor who had achieved fame playing tough gangsters in movies like his then-current hit, *Little Caesar*. More than one newspaper reporter wryly suggested that Robinson might give Capone a few tips on how to behave.

Capone maintained his innocence and kept a cheerful face for reporters, but he was convicted and sentenced to eleven years in prison. The mobster was philosophical about the verdict; he remarked to reporters, "It was my own fault. Publicity—that's what got me. . . . It [the sentence] was a little below the belt. But I guess if I have to do it I can."[31]

Prison

Early in 1932, Capone entered a federal prison in Atlanta, Georgia. He was a model prisoner, although he enjoyed unusual privileges, including expensive cigars, luxury shoes, and uncensored "business correspondence." According to rumor, he devised a system whereby he would knock a tennis ball over the prison wall and another, filled with cocaine, would be knocked back to him.

Clearly, greater security was needed. Capone became, in 1934, one of the first prisoners at Alcatraz Island, a brand-new maximum-security facility in San Francisco Bay. The mobster had few privileges there. He was not allowed radios or newspapers, he could write only one heavily censored letter per week, and his only visitors were two family members per month.

Late in 1939, Capone was paroled after eight years. In part, the early release was because of good behavior. More significantly, his mental and physical health had severely declined. Still relatively young, Capone might have easily resumed his career. However, the once-feared mobster was a ruin.

Sometime in the 1920s, Capone had become infected with syphilis. The disease was not diagnosed, however, until a prison examination. Capone had always been deathly afraid of needles, which may be why the syphilis went untreated.

One manifestation of the disease is sudden, violent mood swings. This may explain Capone's legendary violence—such as the time he murdered two traitors from his organization with a baseball bat at a banquet. Biographer Laurence Bergreen states that the syphilis helped build Capone's reputation: "The Capone we remember was the creation of a disease that had magnified his personality."[32]

The End

The disease was already taking hold as Capone entered prison, and by the time of his parole it had completely invaded his nervous system. His speech was slurred, he suffered from delusions, he shuffled when he walked, and he was only occasionally lucid.

Capone lived the rest of his life in seclusion at his Florida estate, spending his days fishing, playing cards, and passing out sticks of

After parole, Capone, suffering from syphilis, spent the rest of his life at his Florida estate.

gum to anyone he met. Faithful Mae and other family members tended to him around the clock.

The famous gangster died in 1947, of a stroke that led to cardiac arrest. He was buried in Chicago's Mount Carmel Cemetery, ironically also the final resting place of Hymie Weiss and Dion O'Banion—his archenemies from the glory days of bootlegging.

CHAPTER 3

Lucky Luciano: The Organizer

He was born and died in Italy, yet the influence on America of [this] grubby street urchin . . . ranged from the lights of Broadway to every level of law enforcement, from national politics to the world economy. . . . His story was Horatio Alger with a gun, an ice pick and a dark vision of Big Business.

> —Journalist Edna Buchanan

I'd do it legal. I learned too late that you need just as good a brain to make a crooked million as an honest million. These days you apply for a license to steal from the public. If I had my time again, I'd make sure I got that license first.

> —Lucky Luciano, asked late in life
> how he would do things differently

Lucky Luciano was born in 1897 as Salvatore Lucania, the third of five children, in the tiny hamlet of Lercara Friddi, on Sicily, the Italian island where the Mafia originated. His father, Antonio, labored in the village's sulphur pits, but he and his wife Rosalia dreamed of a better life in America. In Luciano's memoirs, he recalls that sometimes the family did not even have enough to eat, because his parents saved everything for the trip to the promised land: "All the time we was growin' up it seemed that all my old man ever talked about was goin' to America."[33]

America

The Lucania family (changed to Luciano in the United States) sailed for New York when Salvatore was ten, settling in the tenements of the Lower East Side. Bored with school and frustrated by teachers who ignored him because he spoke broken English, Luciano attended classes sporadically. Four years after arriving in New York, Charlie as he was called dropped out entirely.

He worked a number of menial jobs, including delivery boy for a hat company. But a life of crime beckoned, and Luciano began gambling and stealing. He also combined his hat deliveries with deliveries for the neighborhood drug dealer, who was connected to the infamous Five Points Gang. When police found a small amount of heroin hidden in a hat box, Luciano spent six months in a reformatory. Luciano refused to name the dealer, however, and so earned a full membership in the gang.

Luciano's father refused to let him return home after his release, and when the teenager was forced to find a place of his own he devoted himself fully to crime. Around this time he met two other teens, Ben Siegel and Meyer Lansky, who were already best friends. The three would form a lifelong friendship.

Luciano was suspected of several murders during his early years, but there was never enough evidence to convict him. This knack for wiggling out of convictions gave him a nickname, according to writer Jay Robert Nash: "His uncanny fortunes with the law coupled to his phenomenal ability to win at craps earned him the name 'Lucky.'"[34]

Charlie Luciano's knack for eluding convictions earned him the moniker "Lucky."

The First Fortunes

Luciano left the Five Points Gang in 1920 to join New York's largest Mafia family, run by Giuseppe "Joe the Boss" Masseria. This connection put Luciano in the business that built his first fortune: prostitution. Jay Robert Nash notes, "From the beginning, women were the tools with which Charlie Lucky constructed his criminal cartel."[35]

At first he sold protection to prostitutes and their madams in return for half their profits. If the women did not go along, thugs in Luciano's employ (never Luciano himself) beat them or destroyed their brothels. Luciano soon branched out into "running" his own women. He reportedly had at one point five thousand women working for him, and by the mid-1920s virtually owned New York's prostitution racket. By 1927, he was making $1 million a year.

With Masseria's protection, Luciano also muscled in on New York's bootlegging and gambling. For the rest of his life, in fact, Luciano listed his occupation as "gambler"—an excellent, and quite legal, front. Unlike Al Capone, Luciano kept the government at bay by carefully filing income taxes every year on the modest money he earned from wagers.

Luciano thrived despite attempts to destroy him by rivals both within and without the Masseria family. The worst of these occured in 1929, when he was abducted and driven around for hours while thugs beat, stabbed, and shot him, then dumped his body. Miraculously, Luciano survived. The attackers may have been connected to another gangster, "Legs" Diamond; it was common knowledge in the underworld that Diamond wanted Luciano's territory. Nonetheless, Luciano refused to tell police who had attacked him, commenting only, "I'm pals with everybody. Nobody's after me. Everybody likes me."[36]

The War Begins

When Masseria's arch-rival, Salvatore Maranzano, declared open war on Masseria in 1930, it signaled the start of a long and bloody power struggle. Luciano was by now Masseria's chief underboss, but he grew impatient with the violent war. Luciano saw the violence as disruptive to business, a pointless battle of egos between the older Mafia chiefs: "To me, the whole thing was a matter of organizin' a business; for them, it was the pride that came first—who was gonna be the Boss of Bosses."[37]

To Luciano, the best way to end it was to eliminate his own boss. He secretly approached Maranzano, received Maranzano's approval, and arranged for the assassination. In April 1931, Luciano took Masseria to a restaurant in a remote section of Coney Island. He encouraged the gluttonous Masseria to drink and eat heavily and dally with a game of cards.

During the game, Luciano excused himself to the men's room. Four hit men, representing four New York gangs, barged into the restaurant and riddled Massaria with bullets. By the time Luciano emerged from the bathroom, the restaurant was filling with policemen.

A truce was signed between Maranzano and Luciano, who took his dead boss's place. But Maranzano was unimpressed with Luciano's ideas for replacing the traditional Sicilian methods with a corporate structure. By September 1932, Maranzano saw Luciano as a threat and put out a contract on the younger man. Crime journalist Edna Buchanan writes of Maranzano, "He found Lucky too ambitious, too enterprising, too dangerous."[38]

The Mustache Petes Go

Maranzano was too late; Luciano struck first, and Maranzano was killed only hours before Luciano's own assassination was scheduled.

Luciano's plan was to eliminate the old-guard mafiosi like Masseria and Maranzano, who were insultingly called Mustache Petes. In his memoirs Luciano recalls, "For us [younger gangsters], rubbin' out a mustache was just like makin' way for a new buildin', like we was in the construction business."[39]

Luciano knew the other Mustache Petes would retaliate swiftly after Maranzano's death. He therefore ordered the deaths of as many as fifty more Mustache Petes within a single twenty-four-hour period. Luciano then arranged to reconcile the remaining older Sicilian gangsters with his younger associates.

In the period after this brutal takeover, Luciano—now without question the top gangster in New York—moved swiftly to organize his syndicate. It was run along established business lines, with rules that required quiet behavior and conservative suits; Luciano joked that it should be on the New York Stock Exchange. "Of course we couldn't advertise with a slogan or a trademark," Luciano recalled, "but that didn't mean things couldn't be run right. So I made up a lotta rules for the guys who worked for me. Why shouldn't I? After all, don't department stores and big offices tell their people how to behave and what to wear?"[40]

Multiethnic Crime

Having secured the cooperation of both old and new Mafia heads, Luciano reached out to non-Italian gangsters. Unlike the old Mustache Petes, Luciano had no problems associating with non-Italians like Siegel, Lansky, or another prominent Jewish gangster, Louis "Lepke" Buchalter. The presence of gangsters from other ethnic groups, Luciano thought, would help reduce intergang warfare.

Luciano named his syndicate the *Unione Sicilione*, in a ploy to appease the remaining Mustache Petes. Luciano himself simply called it "the Outfit." At the top were two dozen family bosses from around the country who essentially formed a board of directors. Non-Italians were accepted as nonvoting members.

The *Unione* controlled not only bootlegging, numbers (a form of gambling designed for poor people), narcotics, and prostitution, but also legitimate businesses such as the waterfront, unions, food markets, bakeries, and the garment trade. About the latter, Luciano, using the slang common in his day, bragged that "every

Jewish gangster Louis "Lepke" Buchalter was an associate of Luciano's.

broad in the United States was wearin' a petticoat I was responsible for puttin' on her."[41]

A subgroup, Murder, Incorporated, became the official assassination group for the national organization. (The name was probably first used by Harry Feeny, a reporter for the *New York World Telegram*.) Approval by the national board was necessary for a hit by the killers, and hits not sanctioned by the board were dealt with severely. An estimated five hundred deaths in a single decade have been attributed to the group.

Despite the presence of multiple directors, there was no question who was the ultimate authority in this ambitious new regime. Journalist Rhymer Rigby notes, "Luciano never assumed the title *capo di tutti capi* ('boss of all bosses'), which he saw as an anachronism, but, unofficially, everyone knew where ultimate power rested."[42]

Living the Good Life

When not assembling his new organization, Luciano lived the good life. He counted famous entertainers like Jimmy Durante, Frank Sinatra, and George Raft among his friends. He owned a stable of prize racehorses. He once invited one hundred guests, including New York's police commissioner, to join him ringside for the championship match between two famous heavyweight boxers, Jack Dempsey and Luis Angel Firpo.

He lived for many years under the name Charles Ross in a suite of rooms at the luxurious Waldorf-Astoria Hotel. He rarely rose before noon, after which he would receive reports from his associates. A chronic insomniac, Luciano sometimes summoned his colleagues to a separate office at the Claridge Hotel, or to a nearby delicatessen, where they would conduct business in the middle of the night.

After work, Luciano would spend hours getting ready for a day at the races and a night on the town, deciding what to pick from the three wall-length closets in his suite. He favored elegant suits, silk shirts, handmade shoes, cashmere topcoats, and expensive fedoras.

Luciano loved to hang out at the racetrack and at swank nightclubs and restaurants. There was always a beautiful woman on his arm, usually a showgirl or a nightclub singer. Luciano was not classically handsome, but many women found him charismatic and interesting. Journalist Rich Cohen writes, "He had a dark fleshy face, curly hair, and a quality smile."[43] A mobster who knew Luciano adds that he was "a gentleman. He'd give a girl a hundred dollars just for smiling at him."[44]

La Guardia and Dewey

Luciano was able to avoid serious aggravation from the law for several years. In the mid-1930s, however, New York elected a new, reform-minded mayor. Fiorello La Guardia, a diminutive but feisty Italian-American nicknamed "The Little Flower," replaced "Gentleman" Jimmy Walker, a charming but corrupt politician who so loved the glamorous club life that newspapers called him "the night mayor."

In 1935, La Guardia appointed a special prosecutor, Assistant District Attorney Thomas E. Dewey, to crack down on the city's rackets. Dewey had already successfully prosecuted a number of top criminals, and now he targeted Luciano as "the czar of organized crime in this city."[45]

Dewey conducted well-orchestrated, highly publicized raids on Luciano's operations, including gambling, prostitution, and narcotics strongholds. Dewey was most successful in breaking up Luciano's prostitution rings, and the district attorney convinced a number of women to testify against the gangster.

These women were at first reluctant to testify because they feared Luciano, but after Dewey guaranteed safety they were eager to talk. Rhymer Rigby comments, "Focusing on the bottom line to the exclusion of all else, Luciano [had long] sought to squeeze ever more money out of the ring, often mistreating the 'dumb broads,' as he called them. [But] Luciano's treatment of the prostitutes proved to be his downfall, when Dewey persuaded a surprising number of the boss's dumb broads to take the stand."[46]

On Trial

New York mayor Fiorello La Guardia.

Tipped off by a sympathetic hotel bellboy that Dewey's detectives were coming to see him, "Mr. Ross" took a sudden vacation, without even packing. Luciano recalls, "I don't remember takin' nothin' with me, not even a toothbrush. I left with only the clothes I was wearin', went down the freight elevator, got in my car, and took off."[47]

The gangster fled to Hot Springs, Arkansas, long a gangland vacation spot and a major gambling center. Luciano thought he would be safe there; the mob had such strong connections in the Arkansas government that he felt New York could never extradite him. After a protracted legal fight, twenty state troopers forcibly removed Luciano from his hotel room to face charges in New York.

The gangster faced ninety counts of extortion and "direction of harlotry"—that is, control of prostitution. The trial was sensational, and newspapers around the country delighted in describing every lurid detail as it was revealed.

Luciano vehemently denied every charge, and his chief lawyer, Moses Polakoff, did a brilliant job of trying to deflect guilt from his client. Nonetheless, in June 1936 Luciano was convicted on sixty-two of the ninety counts. In an ironic reference to the penchant many gangsters have for machine guns, the *New York Daily News* crowed, "DEWEY RIDDLES LUCIANO."[48]

Sabotage

Luciano was sentenced to thirty to fifty years at Dannemora, a remote, bleak prison in upstate New York. He spent his time there reading history and keeping tabs on the empire he had left behind. Meyer Lansky and other trusted associates regularly visited to file reports and accept advice.

Luciano's attempts at parole were turned down year after year—until wartime, when the government needed the gangster's help against its enemies. Edna Buchanan wryly notes, "It took Hitler to win Lucky his freedom."[49]

The U.S. Navy Intelligence Department was increasingly desperate to control security along America's waterfronts. German U-boats off the East Coast, for instance, were sinking merchant ships with disturbing regularity. The navy suspected that the Germans were being given information by Nazi sympathizers on the waterfront. The situation intensified when an explosion destroyed the *Normandie*, a luxury liner being retrofitted for wartime use at a Hudson River dock.

U.S. military authorities were stymied because no dockworkers would cooperate. It was clear that approval from Luciano, still a powerful force despite his imprisonment, would be needed. In a deal brokered by Lansky, Luciano promised to help the government in return for early parole.

The government agreed, on condition that Luciano be deported —that is, permanently exiled—to Italy when the war was over. Operation Underworld, as the deal was dubbed, was approved by none other than New York's new governor, Thomas A. Dewey, who had used his fame from the Luciano trial to reach that office. Lansky told military authorities on Luciano's behalf, "I can promise you one thing. There will be no German submarines in the port of New York."[50]

Deported

Luciano sent word to his people on the docks that they should cooperate. Formerly silent dockworkers, fishermen, and even criminals suddenly became the eyes and ears of naval intelligence. Not long afterwards, eight German spies who had landed in New York were arrested. Caches of explosives, maps and blueprints for sabotage were seized as well.

Later in the war, Luciano was again asked to help the military. Allied forces in Europe needed the cooperation of a powerful Sicilian Mafia leader, Don Calogero Vizzini. An invasion of Italy was planned, and the Allies needed to gather intelligence for their landing in Sicily.

Army intelligence recruited Sicilian-Americans to infiltrate the island, and navy officers reached an agreement with Luciano. From his cell, the gangster arranged for the Sicilian Mafia to assist American agents. With help to guide them over the rugged Sicilian mountains, American forces took the island with great speed; in return, the invaders helped elect mafiosi mayors in several Sicilian towns.

Luciano's lawyer petitioned for his client's release on V-E Day, when the European portion of the war ended. Since Luciano had never become an American citizen, deportation to his native country was a simple task.

The Normandie *(pictured) was one of many merchant ships damaged by German spies during World War II.*

The gangster sailed for Italy early in 1946. Meyer Lansky, who saw him off, reportedly brought two suitcases: one with a new wardrobe and one with half a million dollars in cash. Luciano's stateroom was liberally stocked with the food and liquor he had been denied during his prison years. According to Luciano's memoirs, his associates sent three beautiful women as well.

Exile

Luciano was welcomed as a hero and dubbed *Il Milionario* when he visited his hometown of Lercara Friddi. He then settled in Palermo, Sicily's capital, before moving to Naples and later Rome, living in luxury hotels and making inroads into the local rackets and black markets in each city. But life in Italy was not to his liking, and he arranged to resettle secretly in Havana, Cuba.

In 1947, Luciano convened a meeting there of the Outfit, making it clear that he intended to return eventually to America. So many mobsters flooded Havana that the press took note and discovered that the famous Lucky Luciano was in Cuba.

Alarmed, the U.S. Bureau of Narcotics declared that Luciano was a danger as long as he remained in the Western Hemisphere because of his association with drugs. The bureau suspected that Luciano planned to instigate a worldwide drug-smuggling operation, and—by threatening an embargo of medical supplies—successfully pressured the Cuban government to oust him.

Luciano returned to Rome and tried to pick up where he had left off with his underworld connections. However, the Italian government, embarassed and alarmed by Luciano's earlier takeover of Roman rackets, barred him from the city.

The gangster returned to Palermo and then Naples, accompanied by a mistress half his age, a former dancer named Igea Lissoni, and their two miniature Manchester terriers. Luciano was suffering from heart problems and high blood pressure, and he claimed to be retired.

Death on the Runway

Skeptical, American narcotics authorities kept close tabs on the gangster until the very end. He invested in several local businesses, including a candy factory that allegedly was a front for smuggling heroin into America in candy boxes. He was also a celebrity; Martin Gosch and Richard Hammer, who helped the mobster write his memoirs, note, "Luciano had become the most famous tourist attraction of Naples. Visiting Americans and sailors from the naval base invariably made the California [his favorite restaurant] a place to stop."[51]

Late in life, Luciano developed an interest in making his life story into a film. Luciano's ego had always been strong, and he thought Cary Grant would be a good choice to play the lead. Jay Robert Nash writes, "All that remained for him was a gnawing vanity that insisted his life was worth an epic movie."[52]

Believing Luciano (center) was a threat as long as he stayed in the Western Hemisphere, the U.S. Bureau of Narcotics insisted that he be deported to Italy.

In 1962, while on the runway of the Naples airport to meet with an American movie producer, Luciano died of a heart attack. Edna Buchanan wryly notes, "Unlike so many of his predecessors and colleagues, he expired of natural causes, a coronary—an occupational hazard common to hard-driving executives."[53]

American authorities decided to allow his body back into America, where he had wanted to be buried. He lies in a vault in St. John's Cemetery in New York. Soon after the mobster's death, Italian and U.S. officials announced they had been about to arrest Luciano for conspiracy to create an enormous, multinational heroin ring.

CHAPTER 4

Meyer Lansky: Quiet Banker to the Mob

Trust your memory. Keep your business in your hat.
—Meyer Lansky

Max and Yetta Suchowljansky brought their family from Grodno, Russia, to America in 1911. Like so many Jewish immigrants of the time, they settled in Manhattan's Lower East Side. Their son Maier had been born in Grodno sometime in 1902; the exact date is uncertain. It was probably a customs official who Americanized the spelling of his name to Meyer Lansky.

Life in the crowded streets of New York was tough for an immigrant kid, and fights among gangs were common. Meyer was small, and even as an adult he stood only five feet five inches tall. But he was spirited and fearless, quick with his fists, and showed enormous self-control, secrecy, and determination.

Above all, Lansky was bright. He scored near-perfect grades, solved complex computations in his head, and relaxed by doing mathematical puzzles. He liked to read history

The intellectual Meyer Lansky enjoyed reading and claimed that he had memorized Shakespeare's Merchant of Venice.

47

and could memorize long stretches of literature. As an elderly man, the gangster made autobiographical notes in which he recalls, "We learned a lot of History from Roman to American. . . .Was able to recite [Shakespeare's] Merchant of Venice by memory."[54]

A Chance Meeting

Lansky stayed in school through the eighth grade and found work as an apprentice tool and die maker. He worked fifty-two hours a week, at ten cents an hour, to supplement his father's wages as a garment presser.

But Lansky did not last long at honest work. He began wagering on street-corner gambling—and often won because he could juggle complex math in his head. This led to work as a lookout, alerting gamblers when police were near. In 1918, Lansky was arrested on two occasions for assault and disorderly conduct. That same year he met two teens who would figure prominently in his life: Ben "Bugsy" Siegel and Lucky Luciano. According to legend, all three met on the same day, during a street fight, but this is unlikely. In any event, they were fast friends—especially Meyer and Ben—by the time they were teenagers.

In 1921, Lansky gave up his day job when he and Siegel organized a "floating" crap game. Craps is a gambling game that was popular at the turn of the century. Because it was illegal, games often "floated" daily from one location to another to escape the police.

The two also stole goods from pushcarts, burglarized shops, and collected money for loan sharks. Their protector was Luciano's mentor, "Joe the Boss" Masseria, who kept the police away in return for a portion of the profits.

The Bug and Meyer Gang

Prohibition provided the perfect opportunity for the young thugs to expand their horizons. They gathered around them a group of toughs, the Bug and Meyer Gang, which at first provided bodyguards for bootleggers. The real money began flowing, however, because Lansky, the former tool and die maker, understood a relatively new technology: automobiles.

Using a car-repair business as his front, Lansky could remove serial numbers from or change the appearance of a stolen car, make engines powerful enough to outrun police, or build hidden storage space into an auto. He and Siegel also maintained a fleet of vehicles that they rented to bootleggers. Eventually the gang expanded into full-service smuggling, bringing alcohol in from the Caribbean and Canada. Lansky liked to boast that he ran the world's most efficient international shipping business.

Prohibition made Lansky wealthy, and he moved into the top ranks of New York's criminal class when Luciano's destruction of the Mustache Petes brought a new generation to power. Nonetheless, Lansky mostly avoided the wrath of the government. Arrested on only minor charges seven times as of 1931, he was acquitted on four and paid token fines on the others.

As Prohibition ended, Lansky moved in a direction that had long interested him: gambling. He considered it a clean racket, as opposed to drugs, which he scrupulously avoided. Lansky cultivated interests in dog and horse racetracks, and he opened a series of casinos, called "carpet joints" for their emphasis on elegance, that combined gambling rooms with restaurants and floor shows.

From Liquor to Gambling

In planning his gambling empire, Lansky kept an eye on the big picture. The advantages of casinos in big cities were obvious, but

After Prohibition, Lansky invested in dog and horse racetracks and opened many luxurious casinos.

Lansky saw potential in remote locales. For instance, he developed an operation in Hot Springs, Arkansas, where thousands of people, mostly elderly, came for the medicinal waters. After bathing in the waters, there was little to do—until Lansky introduced gambling. Another advantage to small towns was that local authorities were generally more tolerant of gambling and its accompanying vices.

Typically, Lansky supplied development money for a casino or racetrack but put friends and associates in charge and kept his name off the paperwork. Officially, he was a simple fruit sales-man, and his official employer was his father-in-law.

This connection resulted from Lansky's marriage to Anne Cit-ron in 1929, a union that was at least partly made as part of the gangster's plan to seem legitimate. Anne apparently knew that her husband had some shady dealings, but there was little chance that she would inquire deeply into his affairs.

The couple had three children: Bernard, Paul, and Sandra. Bernard, called Buddy, was born with cerebral palsy. His mental faculties were normal, and he was cheerful and bright, but his physical disabilities worsened as he aged. In time, Lansky would dote on Buddy, spending a fortune seeking medical help for him. At first, however, Lansky went into a deep depression and briefly left the family. "It embarrassed him," biographer Robert Lacey writes of Buddy's birth defects. "Meyer liked to feel that he was in control of things, and if he sensed that this was not the case, he would just withdraw from the situation."[55]

Taking Over from Lucky

In the mid-1930s, Lansky began expanding overseas. He set his sights on Cuba, and spent much of his time in Havana. By 1937, he had control of the casino in the elegant Hotel Nacional as well as the local racetrack, kicking back half his profits to Cuba's dic-tator, Fulgencio Batista. During World War II, however, the stream of wealthy gamblers from America to Cuba dried up. Lansky withdrew from Havana and concentrated on his holdings in Florida.

Lansky's primary concern during the war, as always, was on his business. Nonetheless, he was an anti-Nazi activist both before and during the conflict. Lansky was in a position to muster the necessary muscle and weapons to break up pro-Nazi meetings with fire bombs and beatings. "I was a Jew," he remarked later, "and I felt for those Jews in Europe who were suffering."[56]

He also played a key role in the collusion between Lucky Luciano and the U.S. military. This was a typically farsighted move for Lansky. He knew that whoever freed Luciano from prison would gain status and power within the underworld. Furthermore, Lansky guessed correctly that Luciano would be deported, and, as a trusted friend and associate, he himself would be in position to take over most of Luciano's operations.

The strategy worked. Charles Siragusa, a Narcotics Bureau agent who tracked Luciano for years, noted in an official memo that "Luciano came to an understanding with Mafia elements in the U.S.A. that Meyer Lansky was to supervise all of Luciano's previous racket activities. . . . For the most part, the underworld has abided by his wishes."[57]

Dictator Fulgencio Batista (pictured) benefited from Lansky's interest in Cuba.

Family Life Deteriorates

By carefully laying a solid foundation with such plans, Lansky emerged in the postwar years as the single most powerful man in crime. However, he paid a personal price. Like many businessmen, Lansky put his job before his family. He was gone from New York for long periods, and even when home he was often unavailable. At least in part because of the distance he maintained, life in the Lansky family became increasingly more difficult.

Buddy, by now a young man, idolized his father, loved to hear stories of Lansky's "business" trips, and, as he grew older, began helping Lansky with some of his ventures. But there was no love lost between Lansky and his second son, Paul, whom Lansky was pushing to attend West Point. And Sandy, the youngest child and only girl, was strong-willed, rebellious, and spoiled.

Meanwhile, Lansky's marriage was deteriorating. Anne found it increasingly difficult to ignore her husband's illegal acitivities, and violent fights resulted. "She would throw things at him," Buddy Lansky recalls. "There was hollering, screaming. . . . I used to wake up in the middle of the night and hear them fight."[58]

Anne's mental health had always been fragile, and in 1945 she briefly entered a mental institution for electroshock treatment. She filed for divorce shortly afterward, and the children went to live with her when the divorce became final in 1947.

Lansky apparently did not have a major weakness for women; he considered sex a distraction from business. Still, he had several affairs, both before and after his separation from Anne. None was serious until he met Thelma Schwartz. Teddy, as she was called, was a diminutive, brassy manicurist in the barbershop of New York's Embassy Hotel. The couple was wed in 1948 and wintered in Florida before settling into a penthouse apartment on New York's elegant Central Park South.

Grand Juries

For years, Lansky had been a target of investigations by government agents. During the 1950s, this scrutiny increased sharply.

One of the most serious groups to apply pressure was the Senate Committee to Investigate Organized Crime in Interstate Commerce. This council, known as the Kefauver Commission after Senator Estes Kefauver of Tennessee, was the first large-scale congressional investigation of organized crime in the United States.

Lansky was ordered to testify in 1950, and he made the committee's work as difficult as possible. He appeared without an attorney, refusing to answer questions or produce records about his businesses. Ordered to appear again with an attorney, he reluctantly produced a few records pertaining only to his holdings in jukebox and television companies.

The Kefauver hearings caused Lansky little direct trouble. However, they created publicity, and a number of states began bothersome investigations of their own. Lansky-controlled casinos in Florida were forced to close after it was revealed that a succession of governors had been influenced by mob interests. Lansky and his brother Jake were also indicted by a Florida grand jury investigating an illegal club.

Another investigation concerning the racetrack in Saratoga, New York, led to Lansky's first arrest in twenty years. In the fall of 1952, he pleaded guilty to charges connected to gambling and was sentenced to ninety days. It was the first time the gangster had ever been sentenced to prison. After his release, he decided to move permanently to Florida. He told Teddy he was retiring.

A Low-Key Life

Lansky bought an unpretentious house in Hallandale, a suburb of Miami. The couple's Chevys sat in the driveway, because Teddy used the garage for ongoing sales of her used clothing. They later relocated to an elegant new apartment in Miami Beach.

Lansky's daily routine was as unpretentious as his homes, even in retirement. Driven by a bodyguard every morning to his office in a motel, he would meet with various associates. Lunch was at a famed delicatessen, Wolfie's, and afternoons were usually spent playing cards or golf. He was always home by midafternoon.

A member of long standing of the Book-of-the-Month Club, Lansky spent most evenings at home. He especially enjoyed books of history, biography, and economics. He also enjoyed watching television, especially nature shows, and late in his life was a faithful subscriber to Miami's public TV station. When he and Teddy went out, it was to a nearby Italian restaurant where they always had the same table.

Though Lansky appeared to be nothing more than a mild-mannered retiree, the hard-edged, menacing personality that had served him during the days of the Bug and Meyer Gang occasionally emerged. "He was a cold man, as cold as ice," recalls Buddy Lansky's wife Annette. "He could look right through you. He was intimidating. You didn't know why. This little man—what could he do to you? But you felt afraid."[59]

No Prosecution

In addition to various grand juries, Lansky was plagued by a lengthy Internal Revenue Service investigation. The IRS was hoping

The Justice Department's failure to prosecute Lansky led to rumors that the gangster was being protected by FBI chief J. Edgar Hoover (pictured).

to bring down Lansky the same way it had brought down Capone: by proving income tax evasion. However, Justice Department officials declined to prosecute. Twice, efforts were made by the IRS to reopen the case, but the Justice Department continued to refuse. In 1955, the IRS closed Lansky's file.

Efforts were also being made to attack the gangster on another front. Lansky could have been deported if he lost his citizenship; the Immigration and Naturalization Service hoped to argue that, since he had lied about his arrest record during naturalization proceedings in 1928, his citizenship was invalid.

Like the tax case, however, this was stymied by the Justice Department. The department's refusal to prosecute Lansky led to a persistent rumor that he was being protected by someone high in government. There have been a number of theories about this reluctance to prosecute Lansky, usually involving FBI chief J. Edgar Hoover. Hoover may have been innocent of a cover-up; it is true, however, that for decades the powerful law-enforcement official refused to even admit the existence of organized crime.

Perhaps this stemmed from underestimating the underworld. Journalist Rich Cohen speculates, "Maybe he [Hoover] saw them as little more than brutish thugs, clearly not smart enough to create a national syndicate."[60] Writer Sidney Zion, however, postulates more sinister reasons: "Perhaps the image-conscious FBI chief feared his agents were powerless against the strengthening underworld syndicates; perhaps . . . the gangsters owned damning evidence about the top cop's private affairs."[61]

Though apparently immune from prosecution on the federal level, state authorities continued to dog Lansky's steps. In New York in 1958, the gangster was arrested and questioned about the recent murder of Albert Anastasia, the former head of Murder, Incorporated.

Lansky was booked for vagrancy and spent a night in jail. The vagrancy charge, bizarre in light of Lansky's obvious affluence, was made because police could find nothing else to pin on him. It was justified by Lansky's reply when asked what he did for a living: "Business." Pressed for details, he said only, "My kind of business."[62]

Investments and Banking

Throughout the 1950s, Lansky increasingly acted as a broker, arranging for his associates to provide financing for casinos in Cuba and America. He kept complete control over only one pet project, the Riviera in Havana, although his name was not on any paperwork except to identify him as the hotel's kitchen manager. This and other Cuban operations flourished for several years. However, when Fidel Castro's revolution seized power in 1959, Lansky and his associates were forced to evacuate. At the same time, it was increasingly difficult for Lansky to operate in America. In 1961 the new attorney general, Robert Kennedy, vowed to destroy organized crime. Lansky decided to concentrate on countries where the politicians were more malleable.

All through the 1960s, Lansky successfully developed casinos in the Bahamas, South America, and Hong Kong. He also concentrated on his increasingly important role as banker to the underworld. Lansky specialized in creatively hiding the billions of dollars in mob profits flowing in yearly. He formed his own bank, the Bank of Miami Beach. Cash was often taken by courier from Miami to Switzerland, where it was deposited in untraceable accounts. Lansky also formed a number of foreign corporations through which money passed. When it was laundered and untraceable, the money could be brought back to the United States and reinvested.

Lansky persevered, and by the end of the 1960s the last of his rivals were gone. "Little Augie" Carfano, a longtime rival, was shot to death while trying to take over Lansky's Florida gambling concessions. Abner "Longy" Zwillman, king of the New Jersey rackets, was found dead in his mansion—officially a suicide, although there was speculation that it was murder. And Vito Genovese, who favored expanding the narcotics trade against Lansky's wishes, went to prison, where he died in 1969.

According to biographer Hank Messick, these deaths marked the end of an era for Lansky: "The men with whom he had worked, and sometimes fought, were old, rich, and tired—or dead, deported, or in prison. A new generation was coming along—young men who might be college trained, who carried no criminal record dating back to Prohibition, who had never been arrested for illegal gambling."[63]

Harassment?

In 1970, for the first time in twelve years, Lansky was arrested. A customs check following a Mexican vacation found medication in a nonprescription bottle. Lansky said it was a barbiturate antispasmodic for his ulcers, which had troubled him since the 1940s. However, Lansky did not have a doctor's prescription and so was guilty of a state felony.

The subsequent trial gave reporters and photographers a rare opportunity to record the reclusive gangster. Lansky was acquitted on a technicality, but the trial served its purpose for the government. It occurred in the midst of a campaign to legalize gambling in Miami Beach. The public saw so many headlines linking the words "Lansky" and "drugs" that voters were persuaded to reject the gangster's casino.

Lansky was arrested after a customs check found medication in a nonprescription bottle he was carrying.

Avoiding what Lansky claimed was government harassment, he and his wife traveled to Israel later that year, accompanied by their beloved Shih Tzu dog. They settled in a luxury hotel in Tel Aviv for an indefinite stay, and Lansky applied for permanent residence, claiming his right to citizenship as a Jew.

Although he was never religiously observant, Lansky had been intensely interested in Israel's welfare since the formation of the Jewish state in 1948. He had donated generously to Jewish causes for years, and since his first visit there in 1962 he had loved its climate and lifestyle.

Nonetheless, Israeli authorities refused Lansky permanent status because of his criminal background. According to the gangster's granddaughter, Myra Alverman, this was a bitter disappointment: "One of the biggest heartbreaks of his life was being refused citizenship to Israel."[64]

"Laughing That He Whipped Us All"

Lansky had to leave Israel but was unwilling to return to America for fear of more trials. He considered the South American country of Paraguay but was refused entry there even as a tourist. When he reluctantly returned to America, Lansky was arrested as he stepped from the plane.

His fears were justified, and he was brought to trial over two matters. One was the tax evasion case that had been pending for years. The other was contempt of court, for failing to return from his Israel sojourn to appear before a grand jury. He was sentenced to a year and a day, but appeals kept him free.

Lansky's main argument in the appeal process was his worsening health; he was seriously ill with heart and lung problems. The gangster underwent triple-bypass surgery in 1973 and gave up a lifelong three-pack-a-day cigarette habit. His case, in the end, was dropped. An FBI agent who was involved remarks, "He was able to go to his grave laughing that he whipped us all."[65]

Despite rumors that Lansky had secreted a fortune of some $300 million, the gangster was apparently plagued by serious money problems in his last years. According to some sources, his fortune had never even approached that mythical number, and what money he did have was gone. Late in life, this most obsessively private of men even considered publishing a memoir to raise cash.

For the last decade of his life, Lansky apparently was truly retired. He became a familiar sight to residents of Miami Beach, strolling along Collins Avenue with his dog and bodyguards. He sometimes stopped and waved to the FBI agents assigned to trail him. He collected Social Security, played cards with friends, and napped in the afternoons. Lansky died of lung cancer in 1983.

CHAPTER 5

Ben "Bugsy" Siegel: The Man Who Invented Las Vegas

Ben . . . may have done some wicked things, but at heart, he is a good man.

—Countess Dorothy di Frasso

We only kill each other.

—Ben Siegel

Like Meyer Lansky's parents, Benjamin Siegel's parents arrived in New York City from eastern Europe as part of the great wave of Jewish immigration. They came in 1903, three years before he was born, on February 28, 1906, the second of five children.

The Siegels lived in Williamsburg, a rough neighborhood of Brooklyn that was largely dreary factories and desperately poor tenement buildings inhabited by recent Irish, Italian, and Jewish arrivals. Both parents worked in nearby clothing factories. Journalist Pete Hamill paints a vivid portrait of the neighborhood:

> The tenements were filled with rats and roaches. On summer nights, the poor slept on fire escapes while the foul stench of Newtown Creek stained the air. Horses died in the summer heat; their bodies soon swelled and bloated and kids used them as trampolines. In schools, children had their heads shaved to prevent ringworm and lice. Tuberculosis was everywhere. The centerpiece of most kitchens was a bathtub covered with a metal top. After he became famous, Ben Siegel was said to shower four times a day. But there are some things about poverty that can never be washed away.[66]

Young Ben was bright, and by adolescence he was handsome, with dark hair, blue eyes, and considerable charm. But he also had a temper, and his sudden, violent fits of anger led to his famous nickname: "Bugsy," as in crazy as a bedbug. He developed a hatred for the name, and was known to attack anyone who unwittingly called him that to his face.

Like many tough immigrant kids, Siegel was determined to better himself. He wanted more than what he saw around him, and the easiest path to take was crime. Jay Robert Nash writes, "All about him was corruption, poverty, disease, and early death. As a boy, he vowed to rise above the slums."[67]

Moving Up

There are many stories about how Siegel met his lifelong friend Lansky. The most likely is that both were present when two rival groups of craps players got into a fight. When a gun fell from a gambler's pocket, Siegel grabbed it, leveling it at the weapon's owner even as police sirens were heard in the distance. Lansky grabbed Siegel's arm to make him drop the gun and the two ran to safety. Lansky told the younger man that he should

The temperamental Ben "Bugsy" Siegel saw crime as a way to improve his social status.

never risk being caught with a weapon. Siegel replied only, "I needed that gun."[68]

Siegel and his partner Lansky got out of the slums thanks to Prohibition. According to most accounts, Lansky had the brains and Siegel the muscle. Journalist Pete Hamill writes, "Lansky was not above using violence in those days. But Siegel had a true gift for applied aggression. Any weapon would do: fists, feet, lead pipes or guns."[69]

Like Lansky, Siegel had a knack for avoiding arrest. Arrested in Philadelphia in 1928 for carrying a concealed pistol, Siegel jumped bail. The Philadelphia police sent Siegel's mug shot to New York but somehow never asked authorities there to arrest him. The next year, he was arrested for dealing heroin, but his luck held again; the charge was dismissed for lack of evidence. Siegel apparently knew which politicians and police could be persuaded to drop cases.

Lansky preferred to keep a low profile, but not Siegel. He began to dress elegantly. He acted like royalty in the city's speakeasies, flashing a thick roll of cash and always accompanied by beautiful showgirls. He moved into a suite in the Waldorf-Astoria Hotel, a few floors below another up-and-comer, Lucky Luciano. Pete Hamill notes that by 1928 "the gangster style had been set, and nobody personified it better than Siegel."[70]

Siegel did take a few steps toward settling down. He married Estelle Krakower in a double ceremony with Lansky and Anne Citron; the men served as best man for each other. Biographer Robert Lacey writes, "Bugs and Meyer operated their bootlegging garage on Cannon Street as partners, and they joined forces for their romantic adventures as well."[71]

Siegel bought a home in Scarsdale, an upscale suburb, for himself, Estelle, and their two daughters, Millicent and Barbara. It was a normal life, except for Siegel's job. In 1931, for instance, he was one of the gunmen for the hit on "Joe the Boss" Masseria. According to legend, Siegel was home in Scarsdale in time for dinner.

Going West

Siegel's early career in New York was prosperous, but he hit his stride after leaving the city. He left in large part because of pressure from prosecutor Thomas Dewey and Mayor Fiorello La Guardia. Siegel was under investigation for the murder of Bo Weinberg; Weinberg had betrayed his boss, Dutch Schultz, the so-called beer baron of Manhattan, and Schultz had hired Siegel to kill his former lieutenant.

Siegel was hired by Dutch Schultz (pictured) to exact revenge on the beer baron's traitorous former lieutenant, Bo Weinberg.

Siegel headed west in 1936 or 1937 (accounts vary). California was not the enormous economic power it would become later, and in many ways Los Angeles was still provincial, underpopulated, and isolated from the mainstream—virtually virgin territory for the Mob. Siegel took to the city right away. He loved its bright colors, palm trees, warm weather, and beaches. It also was the center of the film world, which appealed to Siegel's love of glamour. "This was as far from the hard dark alleys of Williamsburg as a man could go," Pete Hamill notes. "Ben Siegel acted as if he'd walked into a dream."[72]

The mobster quickly established ties with the gangsters already there and created new opportunities for himself. He muscled his way into labor racketeering, obtaining a piece of the screen extras' union. He bought into an offshore gambling ship and race tracks in Los Angeles and Mexico. He also began running floating crap games in the homes of Hollywood celebrities.

Siegel leased an opulent Beverly Hills mansion, brought his wife and daughters out, and gave them anything they wanted. He joined an exclusive country club and took up golf. He was rumored to sleep with a chin strap to keep his profile sharp. He dieted, drank sparingly, worked out, and allowed himself one cigar a day.

He also loved to dress well. Even Siegel's underwear was embroidered with his monograms. Historian Robert J. Rockaway notes, "His preferences ran to broad snap-brimmed hats, pinstriped suits with high-waisted trousers and pegged cuffs, exquisitely tailored overcoats with fur-lined collars, hand-crafted shoes with pointed toes, and handmade silk shirts."[73]

Raft and the Countess

George Raft was a famous actor and an old acquaintance of Siegel's. Raft had grown up poor in New York, quit school at thirteen, and worked as a prizefighter, pool shark, and ballroom dancer before finding fame playing tough hoodlums in Hollywood.

He and Siegel had met in the 1920s, and when the genuine gangster came to call on the movie gangster, they became fast friends. According to writer Andy Edmonds, it was a perfect match: "Ben Siegel and George Raft were mirror images of one another. Raft imitated Siegel on-screen; Siegel imitated Raft off-screen."[74]

The two began partying every night, hanging out in legendary clubs and restaurants like the Brown Derby, Ciro's, and El Mocambo. Siegel became friends with celebrities like Cary Grant, Gary Cooper, and Clark Gable. When the gangster's name was mentioned in a gossip column, he was described as "a sportsman"—a polite word for

Real-life gangster Ben Siegel (left) and movie gangster George Raft became great friends.

gambler. Siegel's charm served him well, notes biographer Robert Lacey: "With his dazzling smile and his slicked-down good looks, Benny Siegel became something of a star in his own right."[75]

Siegel's insatiable taste for women eventually forced his long-suffering wife to divorce him. He dated numerous glamorous actresses and celebrities; notable among the long list was the Countess Dorothy di Frasso, a wealthy American who was married to an Italian count. She and Siegel openly carried on a long and scandalous affair.

According to legend, the countess provided Ben Siegel with an unexpected chance to change the outcome of World War II. Before the outbreak of war, Siegel traveled to the countess's Roman villa with her, only to discover that her husband was there—and had already invited two top-ranking Nazis, Joseph Goebbels and Hermann Göring. The impulsive, violently anti-Nazi Siegel immediately announced he would kill both of Hitler's colleagues on the spot. The countess protested, "You can't do that!" To which the gangster replied, "Sure I can. It's an easy set-up."[76] However, the countess convinced him not to kill the Nazis, pointing out the terrible consequences that would befall both them and her husband.

A Bad Rep

Gradually, many people in Los Angeles came to regard Siegel as something more than just a flamboyant, flirtatious playboy. In part because of his openly conducted affair with the married countess, Siegel's reputation—in the gossip columns and elsewhere —began to wilt. Once, it had seemed that Siegel was immune to bad publicity. More and more, however, he began encountering ill feeling. In part, this tarnished reputation stemmed from a ludicrously conceived and highly publicized trip he took in the fall of 1938.

On this occasion, Siegel and the countess set sail aboard a luxurious schooner, the *Metha Nelson*. Their destination was Cocos Island, off Costa Rica, where legend had it that millions in gold from shipwrecks had been buried. Siegel was determined to uncover a fortune in pirate treasure.

The voyage quickly soured, however. Guided by a supposedly genuine treasure map, Siegel and the countess, along with their various attendants, stumbled for more than a week around the island's beaches. All they found were some rusted shovels from an earlier expedition. Disgusted, Siegel ordered the captain to take him to Panama; the countess, angered at Siegel's high-handed behavior, remained on board. Unfortunately, the *Metha Nelson* then sailed straight into a tropical storm, became disabled, and had to be towed by a passing freighter to Mexico.

When the story reached home, the *Los Angeles Examiner* referred to the yacht as "the Hell Ship," reveled in the voyage's comic details, and announced that one of its passengers had been a notorious New York gangster, Bugsy Seigel. Soon after, the *Examiner* conducted a lengthy investigative report on Siegel, intimating that the "sportsman" from the East Coast had a darker side.

Persistent rumors about him began to circulate, including his being heavily involved in the drug trade across the Mexican border. However, the police were stymied in every attempt to catch him in an illegal act; on one occasion, when they raided Siegel's house on a tip that he had stashed stolen perfume in his basement, all they found were perfectly legal canned figs.

Siegel's reputation was irreparably harmed in 1939, when he went back to his old occupation of hit man. A small-time gangster, "Big Greenie" Greenberg, had threatened to turn informer unless the executives of Murder, Incorporated paid him off. After a failed assassination attempt, Greenberg fled to Los Angeles; Siegel was contacted and gunned Greenberg down.

The murder caused a sensation, but Siegel avoided conviction due to a convenient string of deaths, disappearances, and recanting of testimony by key witnesses, as well as payoffs to officials. Though not brought to trial, Siegel was never again welcome in the upper reaches of Hollywood society. Celebrities shunned him, and he was even forced to resign from his country club.

Virginia and Vegas

Siegel's passion for the countess—and for most other women— waned when he met the great love of his life: Virginia Hill, a sexy,

Raft and Siegel frequented famous clubs and restaurants such as Ciro's.

Siegel showered the love of his life, Virginia Hill (pictured), with expensive gifts.

tough-talking woman originally from Alabama. Virginia Hill and Ben Siegel were made for each other. If Siegel defined the swashbuckling, romantic male gangster, Hill was his female counterpart.

When they met, she was already a notorious celebrity on her own in the fast-moving world of Hollywood glitter. They were soon inseparable; the gangster sold his house and moved into Falcon's Lair, Hill's mansion. Siegel lavished gifts and attention on his new love: $43,000 worth of gowns from a single designer; a bracelet and ring worth $19,000; $7,500 for a single night on the town. These were astonishing sums; adding a zero to the numbers would give a rough idea of contemporary dollar equivalencies. "When I was with Ben," Virginia once remarked, "he bought me everything."[77]

Soon after meeting Hill, Siegel discovered what would become his life's other great passion.

Siegel had first seen Las Vegas, Nevada, before the war. In those days, the dusty little town had about six thousand people, many of them descendants of Mormon settlers or the families of construction workers from nearby Hoover Dam. It had a street of brothels, two dude-ranch-style hotel-casinos, and a few cheap hotels and bars where gambling was legal.

Siegel had a vision about Vegas. Where others saw a flyblown desert town, he envisioned a glittering hotel and casino—a pleasure palace like the ones Lansky had developed in Cuba. He knew that the future was bright for such a prospect: population in the west was booming, commercial air traffic was reducing travel time, and hydroelectric power from Hoover Dam made the necessary air conditioning possible. Siegel was sure that his casino would be followed by more.

Some authorities question whether the idea originated with Siegel. Some cite another gangster, Moe Sedway, or Billy Wilkerson, publisher of the *Hollywood Reporter* and owner of Ciro's restaurant. Whether he originated the idea or not, Siegel was undoubtedly the most prominent underworld figure to push for its development. Writer Sidney Zion notes, "Ben Siegel invented Las Vegas, the New Frontier of the Combination. It would destroy Bugsy in the doing, but it would pour money as never before into the coffers of the Mob."[78]

Siegel began investing in a few established Vegas gambling joints in 1945, and persuaded others to join the venture. He even persuaded Lansky to invest, though by all accounts Siegel's old friend was deeply skeptical. "It was in sorry shape," Lansky recalled about Vegas many years later. "Living conditions were bad. . . . Air connections were bad. And the trip by car was bothersome. It was so hot that the wires in the car would melt."[79]

The Flamingo

Siegel began work on his own project late in 1945. Its name, the Flamingo, was his pet name for long-legged Virginia Hill. The project quickly began spinning out of Siegel's control, in large part because unscrupulous workers and suppliers cheated him. Ed Becker, a Las Vegas talent coordinator at the time, recalls, "What made Benny a failure was that he was not a businessman. He knew nothing about construction. . . . He imported palm trees from Hollywood. We understand that these same trees made fourteen trips from Los Angeles to the Flamingo."[80]

The list of problems kept growing. An unusual bout of rain created costly delays. Building materials were regularly stolen, then resold to contractors the next day. The boiler room was too small. The plumbing was substandard. The curtains in the main rooms were flammable. After Siegel decided that the aisles in the kitchen were too narrow, architects reconfigured them at great expense. When he complained that the air conditioners in the hotel's rooms were too loud, they were replaced. The overall construction budget ballooned from $1 million to a whopping $6 million.

Siegel, increasingly jittery, sought additional cash from his investors, but they were growing dubious. Siegel had sworn that the Flamingo would open by the end of 1946; he feared that his investors would dump him if it was not open for the Christmas season.

The Flamingo's grand opening was on December 26, 1946. Siegel wanted glamour, excitement, dozens of movie stars, and crowds of thrilled visitors; what he got was a bitter disappointment.

Comedian-singer Jimmy Durante and bandleader Xavier Cugat topped the bill; not a bad show, but not the best. George Raft was in attendance in the audience, but Raft's career was fading and he was no longer a top draw. Other Hollywood celebrities were there, but only a handful; it was later rumored that the influential newspaper publisher William Randolph Hearst, who hated gambling, had persuaded many to stay away. The hotel portion of the complex was unfinished, so guests who came from Los Angeles returned almost immediately or stayed elsewhere in Vegas. Before the night was over, the dealers outnumbered the customers in the Flamingo's gambling rooms.

Sliding Downhill

Siegel's grand project never regained its momentum. Within weeks, audiences abandoned the showrooms. Silverware and food disappeared from the kitchen. Professional gamblers arrived, not the casual players Siegel sought, and the pros started busting the bank. At the end of the first two weeks, the Flamingo had done the unthinkable: it lost money.

Siegel began sliding into even more frequent rages and irrational behavior. He viciously beat a dealer he thought was cheating. He had to be restrained from assaulting a newspaper columnist who had been attacking him in print. Furious at continuing bad publicity, Siegel chased his press agent around the swimming pool, firing a pistol. Unwilling to tolerate such behavior, Hill abruptly left Vegas and moved back to Beverly Hills. By the end of January, Siegel forlornly joined her, closing the Flamingo so that construction could be completed.

It reopened in March, with Siegel full of hope and new ideas, such as midweek bingo games to draw in locals. However, ideas alone were not enough to convince Siegel's angry investors. Writer Lewis Yablonsky notes, "Siegel had exhausted whatever tolerance or good will his associates had allowed."[81]

The end for Siegel and his dream palace can be traced to the underworld convention at the Hotel Nacional in Havana held by the exiled Lucky Luciano, shortly before the Flamingo's opening. One of the topics of discussion was Ben Siegel.

The charges were grave. The gangsters belived that Siegel was cheating them. They had received reports that Siegel was skimming hundreds of thousands in cash out of the casino's construction fund. There were further reports that Hill had secretly traveled to Zurich, Switzerland, depositing money and buying an apartment there.

Even his lifelong friends could not save Siegel from the path he had chosen. Luciano later remembered the discussion this way:

> There was no doubt in Meyer's mind that Bugsy had skimmed this dough from his buildin' budget, and he was sure that Siegel was preparin' to skip as well as skim, in case the roof was gonna fall in on him. Everybody listened very close while Lansky explained it. When he got through, somebody asked, "What do you think we ought to do, Meyer?" Lansky said, "There's only one thing to do with a thief who steals from his friends. Benny's got to be hit."[82]

The End

On June 20, 1947, Siegel was staying in Hill's house in Beverly Hills. Hill had gone to Europe with a former boyfriend. The mobster spent the day running errands. He went to Drucker's barbershop for a trim, visited George Raft, and met with his attorney and a Flamingo publicist.

On June 20, 1947, Siegel was gunned down while he was reading a newspaper on Hill's living room couch.

Hill's brother, twenty-one-year-old Chick Hill, was staying at the Beverly Hills house with his girlfriend, Jerri Mason. That evening, Siegel took them and a friend, gambler Allen Smiley, to dinner. Back home, Chick and Jerri went upstairs; Smiley and Siegel sat at either end of the living room couch. Siegel read the newspaper. Around 10:30 P.M., someone in the driveway fired nine rounds through the open window with a military rifle. One bullet went through Smiley's sleeve. Six others smashed into Siegel and killed him instantly. Twenty minutes later, two longtime Siegel associates walked into the Flamingo and announced that they were the casino's new bosses.

Despite considerable publicity and a lengthy police investigation, Siegel's killers were never found. Only five mourners attended his funeral: his ex-wife, his two daughters, and his brother and sister. Meyer Lansky denied until his dying day that he had played any role in his friend's death.

CHAPTER 6

Sam Giancana: Chicago Strongman with a Presidential Connection

It has long been a fallacy that Chicago's gangsters . . . were a comprehensive, closely knit organization. Nothing was further from the truth. The gang was nothing but the man who ran it and anyone strong enough to make inroads.

—Biographer William Brashler

As a teen, Salvatore Giancana was called Sal by his family, Sam by his neighbors, and "Mooney," slang for crazy, by his friends. He was the second of the eight children born to Antonia and Antonino Giancana (some sources list the family's original name as Giangana), Sicilians who had arrived in Chicago at the turn of the century. Antonino, a fruit peddler, had settled in a neighborhood called the Patch, a tough neighborhood with a mixed ethnic makeup. Sam Giancana was born there in 1908.

Against the wishes of his family, Mooney dropped out of school after the eighth grade. He held a series of straight jobs but showed far more inititiave as a petty crook: shoplifting, stripping cars, even stealing horses to sell their carcasses for meat. The short, thin-faced, foul-mouthed kid was soon the leader of a gang, the 42s. The origin of this name is unclear; one source speculates that it was in honor of Ali Baba and the Forty Thieves, with two added to make it more powerful.

Giancana was arrested for the first time when he was eighteen and received a thirty-day sentence for auto theft. At the age of twenty, he began a three-year jail stretch for his role in a botched clothing store robbery. For his role in a moonshining operation, Giancana next served time in federal prison from 1939 to 1942. (Though Prohibition had ended, illegal liquor manufacturing was still common.)

Between these jail stretches—the first of seventy convictions—Giancana married his longtime girlfriend, Angeline De Tolve, another child of immigrant Italians. Annette, the first of the couple's three daughters, was born in 1935.

To his wife, and to the world outside the Mob, Giancana was a salesman for his brother-in-law's envelope company. He sold few envelopes, however, and devoted most of his time to small-time lawbreaking. His most notable exploit was part-time work as a wheelman—a specialist in fast getaways—for former Capone bodyguard "Machine Gun" Jack McGurn.

Tests conducted in jail when he was thirty-one years old showed Giancana read at a sixth-grade level. He had a shrewd intelligence, however, and wisdom he had learned in the street. Biographer William Brashler writes that Giancana "had knowledge as profound and sophisticated as any, but it couldn't be learned in a classroom and wouldn't show up in an intelligence test."[83]

The Numbers

Released from the federal pen in late 1942, Giancana returned home to a nation at war. He was not drafted because of his age and because he had two children. Nonetheless, Giancana appeared before his draft board and acted dangerously out-of-control; the board, convinced, ensured deferment by branding Giancana a "constitutional psychopath with . . . strong anti-social trends."[84]

He resumed "work" at his brother-in-law's company as well as his criminal schemes. The most successful involved Eddie Jones, whom Giancana had befriended in prison. Jones was the king of the black criminals who ran Chicago's numbers racket, a gambling scheme aimed at poor people. Giancana borrowed one hundred thousand dollars from Jones, which let the ambitious crook buy into several businesses, including jukebox leasing and a small saloon.

His new businesses thrived, but Giancana, still a small player and a nobody in the underworld, was hungry for more action. In 1946, he executed a bold plot designed to make the Chicago mob take notice: he kidnapped Jones, his former patron, and convinced Chicago's top mobsters that the numbers racket should be mob controlled, with Giancana himself running it. Giancana must have made a convincing argument, because after his release Jones retired—and within a year virtually all of Chicago's numbers action had shifted from black crooks to the Mob.

After this brash move, Giancana's ascent was swift. One of his shrewdest moves was to use the revenue from numbers to finance

Giancana made a name for himself by kidnapping Eddie Jones (center) and asserting that the numbers racket should be controlled by the Mob.

gambling operations in Chicago's suburbs. Giancana saw that the postwar baby and housing booms were creating a population explosion away from the inner city, and he found that many suburban police chiefs and politicians were eager to talk business.

Soon after Jones's kidnapping, Giancana was appointed underboss to Tony "Big Tuna" Accardo, one of the men who had assumed power in Chicago after Capone's departure. Giancana's rise to power was a stunningly fast ascent for someone who had long been a nobody. "Accardo recognized the potential in Giancana," notes former FBI agent and writer William F. Roemer. "This kid seemed to have what it takes."[85]

Bugged

By the early 1950s, Giancana was one of the biggest gambling entrepreneurs in the country and, in 1957, the official head of the Chicago mob. Paul Ricca, Capone's successor and the only man with more power than Tony Accardo, went to jail. Then Accardo, under intense pressure from the IRS, decided to semiretire; he handed things over to Giancana and remained only as an adviser, or consigliere.

Government authorities were watching Giancana closely. For the rest of his life, he would be the object of bugging, wiretapping, and other surveillance by the FBI and other agencies. At first, these investigations did not harm Giancana greatly. Though strongly implicated in several mob-related deaths, no proof connected him. An IRS probe was equally inconclusive. A sixty-seven-count indictment focusing on gambling and conspiracy was brought, but Giancana was acquitted. When the mobster was called up before the McClellan Commission, a federal investigation into organized crime, he "took the Fifth"—that is, he invoked his right, guaranteed by the Fifth Amendment to the Constitution, not to

Hounded by the IRS, Tony "Big Tuna" Accardo (pictured) decided to hand down most of his business to Giancana.

incriminate himself in testimony. As a result, the committee lacked enough evidence to convict him.

Giancana knew he was under surveillance, so his business transactions took place in unbugged places like street corners and cars. When discussion by phone was unavoidable, the mobster was careful to foil wiretaps. Typical was this message: "Go by the Fat Boy's place and pick up six loaves. Take a short one to the guy out west, a long one to the guy downtown, and bring the other four to me."[86] (Translation: collect six stacks of money, then deliver two—one with more money, one with less—and bring the rest back.)

The FBI tracked Giancana physically as closely as they could. For a time, this involved "lockstep," in which as many as twenty agents dogged his steps twenty-four hours a day. Cars trailed him everywhere. Agents teed off on the golf course immediately behind him. "Even when he urinated in public restrooms," writes FBI agent Roemer, "I was right there in the next urinal."[87]

Scandal and Celebrity

The mobster's public face was that of a simple businessman, and the Giancanas were a typical suburban family. The family vacationed in Florida and lived in an unflashy suburban house. Giancana maintained a strict routine, expecting his family to be present and dinner on the table when he got home. The Giancana girls went to the best Catholic schools, and Angeline kept house with almost obsessional care. William Brashler notes that "there was still nothing as important to Giancana as family."[88]

In 1954, Angeline, who had always been frail, died of a stroke. Giancana had always enjoyed the company of women, and after a period of mourning he began dating again. The mobster was ruthless in business and surly to the government agents he came in contact with, but he could also be charming and generous in social situations.

The most significant of his romances was with a famous singer, Phyllis McGuire of the McGuire Sisters. The McGuires had a squeaky-clean image stemming from their church-oriented childhood in rural Ohio; Phyllis recalls, "We weren't allowed to wear shorts or slacks or go to dances and movies, and we had to hide the Old Maid deck when mother came in."[89]

As celebrities, however, the McGuires enthusiastically embraced the world of glamour, and Phyllis's love of gambling led to her meeting Giancana at Las Vegas's Desert Inn in 1960. According to legend, she ran up a debt of one hundred thousand dollars, but a smitten Giancana told the club's owner to "eat" the debt. Writer Dominick Dunne notes that this was "different, of course, from paying the debt, but nonetheless it was a gesture not without charm and romantic appeal, especially since Sam followed it up with a suiteful of flowers."[90]

A romance developed, but remained secret to protect the sisters' image. Then, in London in 1962, Giancana was photographed at a club with a smiling Phyllis McGuire on his lap. The photo, which appeared in newspapers around the world, caused a scandal; for a time, the singers were even blacklisted from clubs and banned from TV.

McGuire was not the only glamorous entertainer Giancana befriended in the late 1950s and 1960s. As he traveled more on "business," he was often seen in the company of celebrities like Marilyn Monroe and Frank Sinatra, and the mobster became increasingly fond of the limelight. As a result, Giancana became—in the 1960s—the most widely recognized underworld figure in the country.

There is evidence that famous singer Frank Sinatra (far left, pictured with the rest of the Rat Pack) functioned as an intermediary between Giancana and President Kennedy.

A Presidential Connection?

Frank Sinatra was the kingpin of a group of friends and entertainers known as the Rat Pack. This group included some of the best-known show-business celebrities of the early 1960s, including singer Dean Martin, singer-dancer Sammy Davis Jr., comedian Joey Bishop, and actor Peter Lawford. Lawford was, at the time, married to Pat Kennedy, a member of the wealthy and influential Kennedy family. In addition, Sinatra was a friend of John F. Kennedy, the dashing young senator from Massachusetts and rising star in the Democratic Party.

Though it has never been proven, a body of evidence points to a direct connection between John Kennedy and Giancana, apparently beginning prior to the 1960 election that made Kennedy president. Kennedy knew the race would depend on a few key cities and states. As an Irish-American, a Catholic, and a Democrat, Kennedy was enormously appealing to the many Chicago politicians and voters who shared those roots. Several sources claim that Kennedy, through Sinatra, asked Giancana to help sway Chicago at election time. Allegedly, Giancana agreed to help; he asked in return that Kennedy, when elected, restrain federal investigations of his business.

However, Sinatra apparently did not have enough influence with Kennedy. After the election, which Giancana felt he had helped make successful, Kennedy betrayed the alleged agreement. He snubbed Sinatra socially; more significantly, he appointed his brother, Robert Kennedy, as U.S. attorney general, and the tenacious Robert promptly declared an all-out war on crime. William F. Roemer comments that a furious Giancana's regard for Sinatra "took a 180-degree turn for the worse when he found out that Ol' Blue Eyes wielded a lot less influence than he thought he did."[91]

Further evidence suggests that, depite this apparent betrayal, a connection remained between John Kennedy and Giancana. Judith Campbell Exner, a Rat Pack hanger-on, claimed in later years that

As attorney general in his brother John's administration, Robert Kennedy (right) fought vigorously against crime.

she was romantically involved with both men while Kennedy was president, and even served as a courier between the two men. It is unclear what degree of relationship existed among the three. However, Giancana admitted his involvement with Exner during the period of the Kennedy administration in the early 1960s, and White House phone logs recorded some eighty calls between Kennedy and Exner during the same period. Journalist Sidney Zion notes, "Exner's story gained plausibility when not even Kennedy loyalists denied her claim of having had a lover in the Oval Office."[92]

A CIA Connection?

In mid-1963, FBI agents monitoring Giancana made a startling disovery: electronic equipment belonging to the U.S. Central Intelligence Agency (CIA) was stashed in the back room of the mobster's headquarters, a nightclub called the Armory Lounge. The CIA is allowed to operate only outside the United States; what was their equipment doing in a Chicago gangster's office?

The official explanation was that the CIA was using gangsters to gather intelligence overseas. It came to light in later years, however, that the story was far more complex. Details of this strange alliance are shaky; apparently, however, the CIA explored the idea of using gangsters to assassinate Cuban leader Fidel Castro.

According to several sources, Colonel Sheffield Edwards, the director of the CIA's Office of Security, contacted an associate of Giancana. Several attempts on Castro's life were subsequently made by a team composed of CIA operatives, contract underworld killers, and anti-Castro Cubans. They used high-powered rifles as well as more exotic methods: cigars coated with poison, toxic toothpaste, even exploding underwater seashells where Castro was skin-diving. Each attempt failed, however, probably because security around Castro was extremely high.

Even more bizarre allegations concerning Giancana, the Kennedys, and the CIA have surfaced in recent years. Giancana's brother and godson, for instance, assert in their memoir that the mobster and the CIA together arranged not only John Kennedy's death but Marilyn Monroe's as well, because she was on the verge of revealing her affairs with both John and Robert Kennedy.

Not everyone believes Giancana had much to do with secret government plots. William F. Roemer, the FBI agent who painstakingly dogged the mobster for years, believes that Giancana simply went along with the CIA to feed his own ego and fool the government: "In my opinion, Giancana's part in the [Castro] scheme was a ruse. . . .What did Giancana have to lose by going along?"[93]

Mexico

Secret plots notwithstanding, Giancana was growing increasingly frustrated with the FBI's constant surveillance. Early in 1963, he took the startling step of suing the agency for harassment, claiming that his civil rights were being violated. No criminal had ever sued in this fashion, preferring instead to suffer government harassment in silence.

The presiding judge ruled partially in Giancana's favor. He ordered a reduction of surveillance, including a ruling that FBI golfers had to stay at least one foursome behind Giancana on the course. However, federal authorities persevered and by 1965 had assembled enough evidence to bring Giancana before a grand jury again on charges of murder, racketeering, and tax evasion.

When the mobster refused to answer any questions beyond his name and address, the judge ordered him jailed until he was ready to talk. It was the first time in twenty years that Giancana had been behind bars. Giancana stayed there a year; the life of the grand jury expired before he agreed to talk, and he was released.

When he came home, the gangster realized that the chances of returning to his former top position were slim. His associates had felt for years that he had been spending too much time with the Rat Pack and Phyllis McGuire while neglecting business, and they were tired of his brutal, attention-getting ways. According to Chicago crime journalist William Brashler, "The antics of Sam Giancana—the court suits, the night-clubbing, the tirades, the entertainers—brought nothing but attention and heat, and business suffered from it."[94]

Sensing the animosity, Giancana stepped down and created a new role for himself: roving ambassador, seeking out

Giancana's associates thought that he spent an inordinate amount of time socializing with Phyllis McGuire (pictured) and the Rat Pack.

new investment opportunities. He began traveling widely, building extensive, Chicago-financed gambling empires in such places as the Caribbean, South America, and Iran.

He also moved to Mexico shortly after leaving prison in 1966. Forming a phony Mexican corporation (since non-Mexicans could not own property), Giancana settled in a plush estate in Cuernavaca, an upscale suburb of Mexico City. Phyllis McGuire was a frequent guest, as were his daughters and many of his old associates from Chicago. When he met new people on the golf course or elsewhere, he introduced himself as retired Chicago banker Sam DePalma.

The End

Giancana looked ready to live out his days in exile, despite occasional speculation that he might return to Chicago. Then, one summer evening in 1974, the gangster was suddenly seized by Mexican agents and taken to San Antonio, Texas, where American officals extradited him to Chicago. When met by FBI agents serving a subpoena for a grand jury, Giancana was still wearing his slippers and bathrobe.

It is unclear why Giancana suddenly became undesirable to the Mexican officials who had long welcomed him. Some sources suggest that illegal payments he made to government officials were about to be uncovered.

Although the aging gangster was under indictment, he was not jailed due to ill health. Instead, he moved back to his suburban house, which had been maintained during his absence by a resident caretaker. Giancana had long suffered from heart and intestinal problems, and now his health began to fail seriously. He spent most of his time in his basement, which had been remodeled to include a den, a dining room, and a kitchen.

In June 1975, Giancana ate dinner in his home with one of his daughters and her family. She left behind the ingredients for one of his favorite meals: Italian sausage, a vegetable called escarole, and some *ceci* beans. Later that night, someone shot Giancana seven times in the head as he cooked this late-night snack. Credit cards and $1,458 in cash were left untouched in his pockets. There were no signs of a struggle, or of breaking and entering. The killer was never found. The FBI concluded that Giancana was assassinated by a rival mobster over his refusal to share his overseas gambling empire.

The Chicago underworld shunned Giancana's funeral. Phyllis McGuire was among the handful of people who attended. She remarked years later, "Sam was the greatest teacher I ever could have had. . . . The two great losses of my life were my father and Sam."[95] The gangster's daughters were among the few others who came to pay their respects to Giancana in his silver casket.

CHAPTER 7

John Gotti:
The Teflon Don

His rise from a tenement to the cover of *Time* is a Horatio Alger
tale, except for the less-than-inspirational fact that his ascent was
achieved via six bullets to [crime boss Paul] Castellano's head.
—Writer Albert Mobilio

If they don't put us away for one year or two, that's all we need.
But if I can get a year run without being interrupted . . . put this
thing together where they could never break it, never destroy it.
Even if we die, be a good thing.
—John Gotti in 1986, in a recording secretly made by the FBI

Little in the early life of John Joseph Gotti Jr., the most famous
living gangster, distinguished him from other crooks who grew up
poor in the slums of a big city. He was born in New York in 1940,
the fifth of thirteen children of an immigrant couple of Neapoli-
tan origin. Gotti's father was a hardworking but poorly paid construction worker, and the family was always struggling.

After the Korean War, when Gotti was an adolescent, the family moved from one blue-collar neighborhood in the South Bronx
to another in Brooklyn. It was here that Gotti joined a teenage
gang and received his early education in crime. Gotti was bright
—he claimed later that he had an IQ of 140—with a barrel-
chested build and a legendary fearlessness. According to one story,
he was so cool that he could walk unarmed into a situation and
convince his enemies to put down their weapons. On the other
hand, he also developed a reputation for hotheaded recklessness.

Gotti's gang was the Fulton-Rockaway Boys, who specialized in
acting as couriers for gangsters who controlled the numbers racket
and in doing other small chores for local hoods. When he dropped
out of school at age sixteen, Gotti had risen far enough to become
the gang's leader. When he was arrested for the first time, at age
seventeen for burglary, he pleaded guilty and received probation.

Hooking Up with the Gambinos

By 1959, Gotti had abandoned his gang to hook up with a much more powerful group: the Gambino crime family. The Gambino clan was one of the most important New York underworld organizations; some authorities say it was the biggest in the nation. It is estimated that the Gambino family at its peak had more than 250 "made men"—that is, full-fledged members—and 500 "associates."

The Gambino headquarters were two modest storefront social clubs, the Ravenite Club in Manhattan and the Bergin Hunt and

John Gotti got his start in crime by joining a teenage gang in Brooklyn before hooking up with the powerful Gambino family.

Fish Social Club in Queens. The Gambinos used them as centers to control their deep interests in such lucrative areas as trucking, construction, trash hauling, labor racketeering, and pornography distribution.

Running a small crew within the Gambinos earned Gotti a good living. He made enough from extortion, truck hijacking, and other rackets to buy a nice house in the Howard Beach neighborhood, several luxury cars, frequent nights out on the town, and a serious gambling habit. Journalists Gene Mustain and Jerry Capeci write, "Gotti was an astounding gambler—losses of $30,000, $40,000, $50,000 a weekend on horse racing and sports contests were common. He once won $225,000 . . . and lost it in two nights of shooting craps."[96]

As he moved deeper into the Gambino organization, Gotti maintained a legitimate-seeming life. His day job was operating a garment press in a Brooklyn coat factory, and he had a family. He married Victoria DiGiorgio, a petite, dark-haired woman, in 1959 and their first child, Angela, was born two years later. Four more children would follow: Victoria, John A., Frank, and Peter.

A "Made" Man

Gotti's arrest record during the 1960s was usually for mundane crimes such as public drunkenness. In 1969, he was jailed for a more serious crime, when he served two years in prison following the botched hijacking of a shipment of women's garments from New York's Kennedy Airport.

Gotti ingratiated himself to crime boss Carlo Gambino (pictured) by killing James McBratney.

A major turning point for Gotti came in 1973, when the gangster earned the gratitude of crime boss Carlo Gambino, the patriarch of his clan. Gotti was one of three men who entered Snoope's Bar and Grill on Staten Island and killed James McBratney, an Irish gangster Gambino thought was involved in the kidnapping and murder of a Gambino nephew.

A grateful Gambino hired a famous lawyer, Roy Cohn, to defend Gotti on the murder charge. Cohn, one of the most powerful attorneys in New York, was a brilliant but sinister lawyer who had risen to fame during the McCarthy-era Communist witch-hunt trials. He was able to reduce Gotti's sentence to manslaughter and arrange a plea bargain. Gotti served two years and emerged a hero to most of the top members of the Gambino family.

He had proved himself a "stand-up guy"—someone who could endure prison without betraying his compatriots. For this, Gotti was rewarded by becoming a made man, and afterwards his star was clearly on the rise. Remo Franceschini, a New York City police lieutenant who has closely followed Gotti's career, remarks, "You could see that he was being groomed for leadership. He had it all—he was smart and he was brutal."[97]

A Penchant for Violence

As Gotti rose within the Gambino clan, he demonstrated a ready willingness to use violence to achieve his goals. He has, over the years, been suspected of carrying out or authorizing at least a dozen murders.

One incident, in 1980, apparently involved revenge for a personal tragedy. Gotti's twelve-year-old son Frank was riding a minibike on his street when a neighbor, a factory worker named John Favara, accidentally struck and killed him with his car. John and Victoria Gotti, who doted on their children, were devastated.

In the weeks after the accident, Victoria Gotti reportedly attacked Favara with a baseball bat, and Favara reportedly received threatening letters, but the mild-mannered Favara did not press charges. Instead, he put his house on the market and planned to leave Brooklyn.

Four months after the accident, John and Victoria Gotti went on vacation in Florida, still in deep mourning. While they were out of town, several witnesses saw Favara grabbed and thrown into a van. He was never seen again. Journalist Peter Maas writes, "The word on the streets of Howard Beach and Ozone Park was that he had been chainsawed to death."[98]

Another example arose in 1984, when Gotti was accused of assault during an argument over a parking spot. Romual Piecyk, a cooling-equipment mechanic, was roughed up by Gotti during the incident, and he pressed charges against the mobster. It was not until later that Piecyk found out who Gotti was. When the case came to trial, the mechanic developed a sudden case of amnesia. He said he could not identify his assailant, although Gotti was in the courtroom. When the charges were dropped, a wry headline in the *New York Post* announced, "I FORGOTTI!"[99]

A Bloody Coup

Gotti rose so quickly within the Gambinos that when his longtime mentor Aniello Dellacroce died in 1985, there was only one person standing in the way of Gotti's ascent to the top. This was Paul Castellano. Carlo Gambino, the patriarch, had little to do with the day-to-day operations, which were overseen by Castellano.

Gotti disagreed with the business strategy of his rival, Paul Castellano (pictured).

Castellano and his chief rival, Gotti, differed on business strategy; "Big Paul" had forbidden trafficking in drugs, something that several family members, including Gotti, had been carrying on clandestinely. Furthermore, the suave Castellano's personal style was worlds away from that of the blunt Gotti, and the two did not get along. Journalist Chitra Ragavan writes, "A thug and a brawler . . . Gotti was nothing like the elegant if equally corrupt Castellano."[100]

Castellano named another man, Thomas Bilotti, as his designated successor, making it clear that Gotti was being passed over. Then, in December 1985, within weeks of Dellacroce's death, Gotti made his move. In the twilight of a Manhattan street crowded with Christmas shoppers, Castellano's car stopped in front of the elegant Sparks Steak House. As Castellano stepped from the passenger door, three men moved in. They opened fire on Castellano and on Bilotti, who was in the driver's seat, before fleeing.

Within days of the hit, which killed both "Big Paul" and Bilotti, Gotti—who said he had been at home at the time—was receiving visits from top Gambino officers and colleagues from around the country. To the FBI agents tracking the Gambinos, these men coming to pay respect indicated clearly that Gotti was being acknowledged as the family's new head.

The Teflon Don

On several occasions from the late 1970s through the 1980s, federal prosecutors tried to put Gotti behind bars for such crimes as racketeering and murder. Their chief tool was a powerful statute passed in the 1970s called RICO (Racketeer Influenced and Corrupt Organizations Act). RICO gave the government the authority to connect two or more criminal acts, such as gambling, and label them a conspiracy. With RICO, investigators had (and have) the legal right to tape telephone conversations, to plant listening devices in cars, and even to bug church confessionals.

Nonetheless, Gotti was able to slip through the fingers of prosecutors time after time. Charges of jury tampering and other forms of intimidation were often made in these cases, but they could not be proved. Because no charges stuck to Gotti, the news media coined a name for him: the Teflon Don.

Gotti's other nickname, the Dapper Don, arose from his vanity. In or out of court, Gotti was always immaculately dressed and barbered. At the Bergin Club, his private offices included a salon where he received a daily haircut and manicure. Gotti also indulged his fondness for hand-tailored suits, expensive ties, and silk shirts. "He looked the way Americans wanted a gangster to look," according to Peter Maas. "It was as if he had studied every gangster movie ever made and absorbed the lessons learned in his own persona."[101]

The bloody coup in 1985 and Gotti's rapid ascent caught the public eye, and within the next few years Gotti became a media star. His brutal charisma apparently appealed to many. There were cover stories in *Time*, the *New York Times Sunday Magazine*, *People*, and the magazine *New York*. The men's fashion magazine *GQ* ran a piece. Newspaper articles on Gotti were increasingly common nationwide, and TV crews, including many from overseas, followed the mobster. Gotti clearly loved the attention; being a famous gangster appealed to his ego, and he often played to the cameras by acting the part of the genial neighborhood boss as he made his daily rounds. Peter Maas writes that by 1989 Gotti "had eclipsed the fame of any Cosa Nostra figure in history, with the possible exception of Al Capone."[102]

1992 Trial

Using the RICO laws, federal prosecutors succeeded in bringing down a number of top Mafia leaders during the 1980s. Among these were Anthony "Fat Tony" Salerno, head of the Genovese family; Anthony "Tony Ducks" Corallo, capo of the Lucchese family; Carmine "Junior" Persico, leader of the Colombo family; and Philip "Rusty" Rastelli, acting boss of the Bonanno family. This string of successes led the government to announce that it had broken the back of the Mafia. Many observers feel that the Mafia, indeed, is today only a shadow of its former powerful self.

By the early 1990s, only one top mafioso in America still walked the streets: John Gotti. That situation changed in 1992, when Gotti was brought to trial on charges including loan-sharking, extortion, and five counts of murder.

His trial was high drama, full of stunning revelations and un-expected turns. The Brooklyn courtroom was packed daily with mobsters, reporters, and ordinary spectators. Much to the defen-dant's delight, the trial even became a star-studded affair; actors Mickey Rourke and Anthony Quinn were among the celebrities who attended, both claiming to be researching upcoming roles. The prosecution in the Gotti case relied heavily on extensive tapes made by secret government bugs. Prosecutor Andrew Maloney, re-ferring to Gotti's self-incriminating conversations caught on tape, told jurors, "This is not a complex case—these defendants will tell you in their own words what it's about. This is a case about a Mafia boss being brought down by his own words, his own right arm and, in the course of it, perhaps bringing down his whole family."[103]

"Sammy the Bull" Talks

The government's star witness was even more electrifying than the tapes. Salvatore "Sammy the Bull" Gravano, a top Gambino lieu-tenant, had been Gotti's link to New York's $10 billion-a-year con-struction industry, and was also closely allied with Gambino interests in food distribution, the garment trade, and waste hauling.

Gravano was originally indicted along with Gotti, but he agreed to testify on the government's behalf in return for having his own sentence reduced. It was one of the very few times that a "made" Mafia figure has broken *omerta*, the traditional Sicilian code of silence that forbids revealing the organization's secrets.

Gravano testified that he had participated in nineteen murders since joining the Gambino family in 1976, and that Gotti had per-sonally approved ten of these "whack-outs." One of these was the coup that had brought Gotti to the top; Gravano described driving with Gotti past the Sparks Steak House, inspecting the carnage, after Paul Castellano was shot down.

Gravano's decision to turn against his former boss sent shock waves throughout the underworld. Jeffrey Toobin, a lawyer who writes about the law for the *New Yorker* magazine, notes, "Sammy's sudden defection and testimony against his former boss still ranks as the most sensational Mob betrayal in history."[104]

Still another blow was dealt Gotti when the presiding judge, Leo Glasser, banned the gangster's lawyer, Bruce Cutler, from the proceedings. Cutler had become increasingly disruptive and contemptuous of the courtroom proceedings. Gotti was forced to hire other, less effective, lawyers for the remainder of the trial.

The combination of the wiretaps, Gravano's testimony, and the loss of Cutler proved fatal, and the jury voted to put Gotti behind bars for the rest of his life. Peter Maas writes, "On April 2, after only thirteen hours of deliberation, the jury found Gotti guilty of all the racketeering and murder counts against him. . . . Both Gotti and [codefendant Frank] Locascio received life sentences without parole."[105]

Top Gambino lieutenant "Sammy the Bull" Gravano shocked the world when he testified against Gotti.

Neighborhood Hero

Some authorities on organized crime had long been contemptuous of Gotti, whom they saw as little more than a vicious, opportunistic thug. The only reason Gotti got to the top, they say, was his brutal use of violence, not intelligence. Many average New Yorkers also remain disdainful of the mobster, feeling he is an unworthy successor to underworld figures from past times. One anonymous longtime Brooklyn resident says, "He's a punk! He doesn't carry the mystique that the old gangsters did at all."[106]

Many news reporters and average New Yorkers, however, considered Gotti a harassed underdog, or even a folk hero. Sensational tabloid media claimed he was a gifted entrepreneur and risk taker; one paper even suggested that he be named superintendent of schools. During his trials, the gangster received thousands of letters from women and other sympathizers who admired him.

John A. Gotti became head of the Gambino family after his father was sentenced to life imprisonment.

Feelings of support were especially strong in Gotti's home neighborhood of Howard Beach and in adjacent Ozone Park, where the Bergin Hunt and Fish Social Club was located. During his final trial, for instance, Gotti's neighbors tied yellow ribbons to the telephone poles, trees, and doorknobs of houses, signaling their desire that he come home a free man.

To most of his neighbors, Gotti was a benevolent leader who took care of problems, watched out for the welfare of the neighborhood, and hurt only those who tried to hurt him. He was generous in his donations to local causes, staged a legendary free Fourth of July feast and fireworks display, and never caused harm. "Half the neighborhood works for him," one neighbor claimed at the time of Gotti's trials. "People have more problems with parking than they have with Gotti."[107] Another neighbor remarked, "If he can, he'll help you out. Everybody listens to him."[108]

Junior's Trial

Gotti's son, John A. Gotti, known as Junior, did not attend the trial that put his father behind bars for good. Gotti had instead ordered his son to rally supporters outside the courthouse. When the life sentence was handed down, some one thousand demonstrators rioted, smashing windows, knocking down barricades, and overturning police cars.

After the trial, Junior assumed control as the head of the Gambino family. However, by all accounts, Junior is not the charismatic and effective leader his father was. One anonymous law enforcement official scoffs, "At least the father was a real mobster; the son's just a token boss."[109]

In 1998, Junior and thirty-nine associates were charged with an array of crimes, including extortion, loan-sharking, gambling, and labor racketeering. In April of 1999, he agreed to a plea bargain that included payment of $1 million in penalties. A jail sentence for Junior is pending. If convicted, he could be sent away for as long as twenty years.

Late in 1998, meanwhile, the elder Gotti was diagnosed with throat cancer. He was transferred from the maximum-security federal penitentiary in Marion, Illinois, to a federal prison hospital in Springfield, Missouri, for treatment.

The New Gangsters

In some ways, the underworld is not as powerful as it once was, thanks to recent RICO crackdowns on the major crime families. Thousands of gangsters are in jail as a result of these investigations, including virtually all of the most powerful Mafia figures. Writing in 1999, journalist Chitra Ragavan noted, "Thirteen years after a federal jury in New York convicted the 'commission' of La Cosa Nostra—the Mafia's board of directors—of racketeering and a raft of other felonies, the storied [legendary] crime syndicate is a shadow of its former self."[110]

In other ways, however, the underworld is more powerful than ever—but in new and different directions. In particular, recent waves of immigrants have contributed fresh blood to the established criminal underground.

Ethnic diversity was always a hallmark of organized crime in America. One unofficial social law for the newcomers to America, only partly a bitter joke, was that "the first generation gets along, the second generation gets honor, and the third generation gets honest." Irish, Italian, and Jewish criminals once were the kings of organized crime—before they became respectable like the rest of their brethren.

Today, ethnic diversity marks organized crime in the same way, reflecting an upsurge in immigration from Asia, Latin America, and elsewhere. Recently arrived Russians, Latinos, Vietnamese, and Chinese have done as earlier immigrants did: they have branched out from their ethnic neighborhoods into the mainstream. Most of this branching out has been legitimate, of course, but part of it has been through criminal enterprise, and as the influence of the old crime families has waned, new ones have stepped in.

Colombians and other groups from Central and South America, for instance, have taken control of much of America's cocaine traffic. Another aspect of the drug trade—the heroin connection—is largely controlled by Chinese and Vietnamese gangs. Russian and Israeli emigrés have muscled their way into a number of lucrative rackets, often specializing in computer-related white-collar crimes. Jamaican "posses" run much of the crack trade. And all of these groups are armed with firepower that the gangsters from the old days could only dream about.

Taken together, these groups threaten to make the Mafia irrelevant, merely a quaint part of history. Attorney and journalist Jeffrey Toobin writes, "Hype and screenplays inflated the reputation of La Cosa Nostra long after these successful [RICO] prosecutions and, more important, demographic shifts rendered the 'made guys' nearly irrelevant. It's the Colombians, the Chinese, and the Russians who matter now—along with such up-and-coming exotics as the Hasidim, the Vietnamese, and the Sikhs."[111]

Numerous gangsters have ended up in prison thanks to federal crackdowns.

However, the resiliency of the older gangsters should not be underestimated. Much of organized crime's estimated $100 billion yearly in untaxed profits still goes to branches of the established syndicate. The Mafia still controls its deeply vested interests in gambling, which it now euphemistically calls "gaming-related entertainment experiences." It is also still the only major crime group that has infiltrated hundreds of legitimate U.S. industries and labor unions. Furthermore, it is aggressively seeking new, high-tech sources of income, such as telecommunications fraud and stock fraud. This established syndicate and the newer cartels together create a formidable system of criminal enterprises. The day of the swashbuckling gangster may be over, but the era of organized crime is not.

NOTES

Introduction: Six Bosses

1. Albert Mobilio, "Made Men of Letters: Our Thing About the Cosa Nostra," *Harper's*, October 1997, p. 68+.

2. Mobilio, "Made Men of Letters," p. 68.

3. Sidney Zion, *Loyalty and Betrayal: The Story of the American Mob*. San Francisco: HarperCollins, 1994.

4. Robert J. Schoenberg, *Mr. Capone*. New York: Morrow, 1992, p. 8.

5. Rhymer Rigby, "Uniting the Franchises of Crime," *Management Today*, March 1999, p. 108+.

6. Pete Hamill, "Bugsy Siegel's Fabulous Dream," *Playboy*, February 1992, p. 104+.

7. Hamill, "Bugsy Siegel's Fabulous Dream."

8. Quoted in David Ellis, "Double Cross," *Time*, April 13, 1992, p. 65.

9. Quoted in Richard Behar, "An Offer They Can't Refuse," *Time*, November 25, 1991, p. 66+.

Chapter 1: The Rise of the American Gangster

10. Robert A. Rockaway, *But—He Was Good to His Mother: The Lives and Crimes of Jewish Gangsters*. Jerusalem, Israel: Gefen, 1993, p. 87.

11. Jill Jonnes, "Founding Father: One Man Invented the Modern Narcotics Industry," *American Heritage*, February/March 1993, p. 48+.

12. Jack Kelly, "Gangster City," *American Heritage*, April 1995, p. 65+.

13. Zion, *Loyalty and Betrayal*.

14. Quoted in Hamill, "Bugsy Siegel's Fabulous Dream," p. 104.

15. Quoted in Mobilio, "Made Men of Letters."

Chapter 2: Al Capone: The King of Chicago

16. Quoted in Zion, *Loyalty and Betrayal*.

17. Quoted in Kelly, "Gangster City."

18. Quoted in Laurence Bergreen, *Capone: The Man and the Era*. New York: Simon & Schuster, 1994, p. 89.

19. Quoted in Martin A. Gosch and Richard Hammer, *The Last Testament of Lucky Luciano.* Boston: Little, Brown, 1974, p. 81.

20. Quoted in Bergreen, *Capone*, pp. 158–59.

21. Quoted in Schoenberg, *Mr. Capone*, p. 290.

22. Michael Woodiwiss, "Capone to Kefauver," *History Today*, June 1987, p. 8+.

23. Zion, *Loyalty and Betrayal.*

24. Schoenberg, *Mr. Capone*, p. 96.

25. Quoted in Zion, *Loyalty and Betrayal.*

26. Quoted in Schoenberg, *Mr. Capone*, p. 292.

27. Quoted in Schoenberg, *Mr. Capone*, p. 212.

28. Quoted in Jay Robert Nash, *Bloodletters and Badmen.* New York: M. Evans, 1995, p. 443.

29. Woodiwiss, "Capone to Kefauver."

30. Eliot Ness and Oscar Fraley, *The Untouchables.* Mattituck, NY: American Reprint, 1976, p. 9.

31. Quoted in Schoenberg, *Mr. Capone*, p. 326.

32. Bergreen, *Capone*, p. 46.

Chapter 3: Lucky Luciano: The Organizer

33. Quoted in Gosch and Hammer, *The Last Testament of Lucky Luciano*, p. 3.

34. Nash, *Bloodletters and Badmen*, p. 397.

35. Nash, *Bloodletters and Badmen*, p. 397.

36. Quoted in Rich Cohen, *Tough Jews.* New York: Simon & Schuster, 1998, p. 60.

37. Quoted in Gosch and Hammer, *The Last Testament of Lucky Luciano*, p. 88.

38. Edna Buchanan, "Criminal Mastermind—Lucky Luciano," *Time*, December 7, 1998, p. 130+.

39. Quoted in Gosch and Hammer, *The Last Testament of Lucky Luciano*, p. 101.

40. Quoted in Gosch and Hammer, *The Last Testament of Lucky Luciano*, p. 70.

41. Quoted in Gosch and Hammer, *The Last Testament of Lucky Luciano*, p. 78.

42. Rigby, "Uniting the Franchises of Crime."

43. Cohen, *Tough Jews*, p. 59.

44. Quoted in Buchanan, "Criminal Mastermind—Lucky Luciano."

45. Quoted in Buchanan, "Criminal Mastermind—Lucky Luciano."

46. Rigby, "Uniting the Franchises of Crime."

47. Quoted in Gosch and Hammer, *The Last Testament of Lucky Luciano*, p. 195.

48. Quoted in Cohen, *Tough Jews*, p. 173.

49. Buchanan, "Criminal Mastermind—Lucky Luciano."

50. Quoted in Cohen, *Tough Jews*, p. 193.

51. Gosch and Hammer, *The Last Testament of Lucky Luciano*, p. 380.

52. Nash, *Bloodletters and Badmen*, p. 403.

53. Buchanan, "Criminal Mastermind—Lucky Luciano."

Chapter 4: Meyer Lansky: Quiet Banker to the Mob

54. Quoted in Robert Lacey, *Little Man: Meyer Lansky and the Gangster Life*. Boston: Little, Brown, 1991, p. 23.

55. Lacey, *Little Man*, p. 70.

56. Quoted in Rockaway, *But—He Was Good to His Mother*, pp. 225–26.

57. Quoted in Hank Messick, *Lansky*. New York: G.P. Putnam, 1971, p. 138.

58. Quoted in Lacey, *Little Man*, p. 130.

59. Quoted in Lacey, *Little Man*, p. 264.

60. Cohen, *Tough Jews*, p. 135.

61. Zion, *Loyalty and Betrayal*.

62. Quoted in Lacey, *Little Man*, p. 242.

63. Messick, *Lansky*, p. 222.

64. Quoted in Zion, *Loyalty and Betrayal*.

65. Quoted in Lacey, *Little Man*, p. 382.

Chapter 5: Ben "Bugsy" Siegel: The Man Who Invented Las Vegas

66. Hamill, "Bugsy Siegel's Fabulous Dream."

67. Nash, *Bloodletters and Badmen*, p. 564.

68. Quoted in Lacey, *Little Man*, p. 34.

69. Hamill, "Bugsy Siegel's Fabulous Dream."

70. Hamill, "Bugsy Siegel's Fabulous Dream."

71. Lacey, *Little Man*, p. 68.

72. Hamill, "Bugsy Siegel's Fabulous Dream."

73. Rockaway, *But—He Was Good to His Mother*, p. 158.

74. Andy Edmonds, *Bugsy's Baby: The Secret Life of Mob Queen Virginia Hill*. New York: Carol Publishing, 1993, p. 84.

75. Lacey, *Little Man*, pp. 151–52.

76. Quoted in Lacey, *Little Man*, p. 112.

77. Quoted in Edmonds, *Bugsy's Baby*, p. 184.

78. Zion, *Loyalty and Betrayal*.

79. Quoted in Rockaway, *But—He Was Good to His Mother*, p. 160.

80. Quoted in Zion, *Loyalty and Betrayal*.

81. Lewis Yablonsky, *George Raft*. New York: McGraw-Hill, 1974, p. 194.

82. Quoted in Gosch and Hammer, *The Last Testament of Lucky Luciano*, p. 317.

Chapter 6: Sam Giancana: Chicago Strongman with a Presidential Connection

83. William Brashler, *The Don: The Life and Death of Sam Giancana*. New York: Harper & Row, 1977, p. 88.

84. Quoted in Brashler, *The Don*, p. 94.

85. William F. Roemer Jr., *Accardo: The Genuine Godfather*. New York: Donald I. Fine, 1995, p. 144.

86. Quoted in Sam and Chuck Giancana, *Double Cross: The Explosive, Inside Story of the Mobster Who Controlled America*. New York: Warner Books, 1992, p. 172.

87. Roemer, *Accardo*, p. 260.

88. Brashler, *The Don*, p. 228.

89. Quoted in David Hutchings, "The McGuire Sisters, Those Sugartime Princesses of Pop, Have Reunited After a 17-Year Split," *People Weekly*, March 3, 1986, p. 46+.

90. Dominick Dunne, "The Biggest Jewels in Las Vegas," *Vanity Fair*, January 1989, p. 124+.

91. William F. Roemer Jr., *Roemer: Man Against the Mob*. New York: Donald I. Fine, 1989, p. 189.

92. Zion, *Loyalty and Betrayal.*

93. Roemer, *Roemer*, p. 157.

94. Quoted in Roemer, *Accardo*, p. 344.

95. Quoted in Dunne, "The Biggest Jewels in Las Vegas."

Chapter 7: John Gotti: The Teflon Don

96. Gene Mustain and Jerry Capeci, *Mob Star: The Story of John Gotti*. New York: Franklin Watts, 1988, p. 13.

97. Quoted in Ken Gross, "Cold-Blooded King of a Hill Under Siege," *People Weekly*, March 27, 1989, p. 70+.

98. Peter Maas, *Underboss: Sammy the Bull Gravano's Story of Life in the Mafia*. New York: HarperCollins, 1997, p. 162.

99. Quoted in Mustain and Capeci, *Mob Star*, p. 37.

100. Chitra Ragavan, "The Son of Don Tries His Luck," *U.S. News & World Report*, April 12, 1999, p. 26+.

101. Maas, *Underboss*, p. 213.

102. Maas, *Underboss*, p. 250.

103. Quoted in Ragavan, "The Son of Don Tries His Luck."

104. Jeffrey Toobin, "Weak Chin," *New Yorker*, August 4, 1997, p. 37+.

105. Maas, *Underboss*, p. 296.

106. Interview with the author, Seattle, WA, July 22, 1999.

107. Quoted in Scott Steele and Bruce Wallace, "Mob Justice in New York City," *Maclean's*, April 6, 1992, p. 26+.

108. Quoted in Steele and Wallace, "Mob Justice in New York City."

109. Quoted in Ragavan, "The Son of Don Tries His Luck."

Epilogue: The New Gangsters

110. Ragavan, "The Son of Don Tries His Luck."

111. Toobin, "Weak Chin."

FOR FURTHER READING

Fred J. Cook, *Mob, Inc.* New York: Franklin Watts, 1977. Written by an investigative reporter, this book is a good introduction to the world of organized crime.

William Helmer with Rick Mattix, *Public Enemies: America's Criminal Past, 1919–1940.* New York: Checkmark Books, 1998. Although not written specifically for young adults, this clearly written account of the underworld's development is informative and well presented.

David C. King, *Al Capone and the Roaring Twenties.* Woodbridge, CT: Blackbirch Press, 1999. A concise and clearly written biography of the notorious gangster and his times.

Gene Mustain and Jerry Capeci, *Mob Star: The Story of John Gotti.* New York: Franklin Watts, 1988. This biography has a more recent paperback sequel by the same authors: *Gotti: Rise and Fall.*

Patrick J. Ryan, *Organized Crime: A Reference Handbook.* Santa Barbara, CA: ABC-CLIO, 1995. Though not specifically for young adults, this is a good, in-depth reference guide to the subject.

Josh Wilker, *Organized Crime.* Philadephia: Chelsea House, 1999. An introduction to the people and issues of the Mob.

ADDITIONAL WORKS CONSULTED

Books

Laurence Bergreen, *Capone: The Man and the Era*. New York: Simon & Schuster, 1994. An excellent book, the definitive Capone story, by a distinguished biographer of prominent American figures.

William Brashler, *The Don: The Life and Death of Sam Giancana*. New York: Harper & Row, 1977. This book, though unsatisfactory in some ways, is still the most complete single biography so far of the Chicago gangster.

Rich Cohen, *Tough Jews*. New York: Simon & Schuster, 1998. A melodramatic but illuminating and fascinating book about the top Jewish gangsters.

John H. Davis, *Mafia Dynasty*. New York: HarperPaperbacks, 1993. A history of the Gambino family.

Andy Edmonds, *Bugsy's Baby: The Secret Life of Mob Queen Virginia Hill*. New York: Carol Publishing, 1993. A somewhat sensationalistic biography of Ben Siegel's great love.

Sam and Chuck Giancana, *Double Cross: The Explosive, Inside Story of the Mobster Who Controlled America*. New York: Warner Books, 1992. A highly speculative book about Sam Giancana by his godson and his brother.

Martin A. Gosch and Richard Hammer, *The Last Testament of Lucky Luciano*. Boston: Little, Brown, 1974. A "memoir" partially dictated by Luciano to a movie producer who was planning to film his life. Highly unreliable, but engrossing because it is one of the few instances of a first-person reminiscence by a top gangster.

Robert Lacey, *Little Man: Meyer Lansky and the Gangster Life*. Boston: Little, Brown, 1991. An excellent biography of the notorious Jewish gangster.

Peter Maas, *Underboss: Sammy the Bull Gravano's Story of Life in the Mafia*. New York: HarperCollins, 1997. A fascinating book, by a veteran crime journalist, telling the story of the man who ratted on John Gotti.

Hank Messick, *Lansky*. New York: G. P. Putnam, 1971. An out-of-date but useful biography of the reclusive Jewish mobster by an investigative reporter.

Jay Robert Nash, *Bloodletters and Badmen*. New York: M. Evans, 1995. A somewhat unreliable but still fascinating compendium of two centuries of American criminals.

Eliot Ness and Oscar Fraley, *The Untouchables*. Mattituck, NY: American Reprint, 1976. Reprint of a 1957 memoir by the famous crime buster.

Robert A. Rockaway, *But—He Was Good to His Mother: The Lives and Crimes of Jewish Gangsters*. Jerusalem, Israel: Gefen, 1993. Written by an American scholar living in Israel, this slim book traces the story of Jewish hoodlums, including Ben Siegel and Meyer Lansky.

William F. Roemer Jr., *Accardo: The Genuine Godfather*. New York: Donald I. Fine, 1995. The former FBI agent focuses in this book on Tony "Big Tuna" Accardo, a longtime associate (and enemy) of Sam Giancana.

William F. Roemer Jr., *Roemer: Man Against the Mob*. New York: Donald I. Fine, 1989. A memoir by a longtime FBI agent in charge of investigating Chicago mob boss Sam Giancana.

Robert J. Schoenberg, *Mr. Capone*. New York: Morrow, 1992. A good, detailed biography of America's most famous gangster.

Lewis Yablonsky, *George Raft*. New York: McGraw-Hill, 1974. Biography of the movie star and friend of Ben Siegel.

Sidney Zion, *Loyalty and Betrayal: The Story of the American Mob*. San Francisco: HarperCollins, 1994. Mostly photographic with brief texts, this is a companion to the Fox TV special of the same name.

Periodicals

Richard Behar, "An Offer They Can't Refuse," *Time*, November 25, 1991.

Richard Behar, "The Underworld Is Their Oyster," *Time*, September 3, 1990.

Edna Buchanan, "Criminal Mastermind—Lucky Luciano," *Time*, December 7, 1998.

Dominick Dunne, "The Biggest Jewels in Las Vegas," *Vanity Fair*, January 1989.

David Ellis, "Double Cross," *Time*, April 13, 1992.

Ken Gross, "Cold-Blooded King of a Hill Under Siege," *People Weekly*, March 27, 1989.

Pete Hamill, "Bugsy Siegel's Fabulous Dream," *Playboy*, February 1992.

David Hutchings, "The McGuire Sisters, Those Sugartime Princesses of Pop, Have Reunited After a 17-Year Split," *People Weekly*, March 3, 1986.

Jill Jonnes, "Founding Father: One Man Invented the Modern Narcotics Industry," *American Heritage*, February/March 1993.

Jack Kelly, "Gangster City," *American Heritage*, April 1995.

Albert Mobilio, "Made Men of Letters: Our Thing About the Cosa Nostra," *Harper's*, October 1997.

Chitra Ragavan, "The Son of Don Tries His Luck," *U.S. News & World Report*, April 12, 1999.

Rhymer Rigby, "Uniting the Franchises of Crime," *Management Today*, March 1999.

Mary Simons, Daniele Billitteri, and Enrico Ferorelli, "A Wounded Mafia: The Latest Chapter in a Long and Bloody History," *Life*, March 1985.

Liz Smith, "The Exner Files," *Vanity Fair*, January 1997.

Scott Steele and Bruce Wallace, "Mob Justice in New York City," *Maclean's*, April 6, l992.

Peter Stoler and Patricia Blake, "The Sicilian Connection," *Time*, October 15, 1984.

Time, "Camelot's seemy side: JFK friend Judith Campbell Exner arranged meetings between Mafia and Kennedy," February 29, 1988.

Time, "Meyer Lansky," January 24, 1983.

Time, "Seems Like Old Crimes," January 2, 1989.

Jeffrey Toobin, "Weak Chin," *New Yorker*, August 4, 1997.

Michael Woodiwiss, "Capone to Kefauver," *History Today*, June, 1987.

INDEX

PICTURE CREDITS

ABOUT THE AUTHOR

Adam Woog is the author of many books for adults and young adults, including *The Importance of Harry Houdini* for Lucent Books. He lives in his hometown, Seattle, Washington, with his wife and young daughter.